# Auntie Mom

### A Single Woman's
### Unexpected Adventure into Motherhood

## LAURA MAHER

iUniverse, Inc.
Bloomington

Auntie Mom
A Single Woman's Unexpected Adventure into Motherhood

*iUniverse books may be ordered through booksellers or by contacting:*

*iUniverse*
*1663 Liberty Drive*
*Bloomington, IN 47403*
*www.iuniverse.com*
*1-800-Authors (1-800-288-4677)*

ISBN: 978-1-4620-3401-7 (sc)
ISBN: 978-1-4620-3402-4 (e)

Library of Congress Control Number: 2011911031

*Printed in the United States of America*

*iUniverse rev. date: 12/30/2011*

*Author's Note:*

The stories and events in this book are true. To respect the privacy of some of the characters, I have chosen to change the names of those individuals. I have also occasionally altered or merged characters and events to simplify the reading of this book.

To my precious little ones, who are not so little any longer. You have shown me the way into my heart. Hopefully I have become a better person.

The best and most beautiful things in the world
Cannot be seen or even touched.
They must be felt with the heart.

—Helen Keller

Christmas in Los Angeles

# Introduction

I KNEW THINGS WERE FALLING APART, even though I lived three thousand miles away. She called me drunk late at night every once in a while. It was her way of reaching out. But I refused to take her calls. I'd been building a new life for myself over the past few years since I moved away. I had stopped drinking. I had put myself into therapy. I had even fallen in love and was happily engaged to be married again. My life finally had a soft, easeful rhythm after years of tension and struggle. I didn't want to be pulled back into my old, messy life.

Besides, how bad could things really get?

One night, years before, when we had had a few too many drinks, my sister asked me if I'd be there for her, for her kids, if anything ever happened to her.

"Of course I'll be there. You can count on me," is what I told her. And I meant it…then.

# May 1996
## The Call

The scorching heat of the L.A. sun formed a misty haze across the distant ocean horizon. From the top ridge of the canyon we could hear the steady echoing hum of the freeway traffic from the valley below. Steve, my fiancé, and I were lounging by the pool, sitting side by side on white recliners under a scarlet floral sun umbrella. Steve was reading the latest baseball news in the *Sunday Times*. I was eating a salad, with my nose buried in a book. We had just returned from church service and planned to spend the day relaxing at home.

The house phone rang. Expecting a call, Steve jumped up to grab it, quickly dashing off into the house. Moments later he reappeared in the doorway.

"Sweetheart, it's your dad," he hollered, waving the cordless phone in the air.

*Strange*, I thought, as I placed the book on the cushion, *we just talked a few days ago. Must be important.* With the salad in my hand, I walked over toward the shaded arched doorway. Smiling, Steve handed me the phone, then leaned over, gently kissing my cheek before disappearing back out into the sunlight.

"Hey, Dad."

"Hi, dear. How are you?"

"Good. Steve and I are hanging out by the pool. We're waiting for the heat to cool down before we take a late afternoon hike." I walked into the kitchen and placed the salad bowl on top of the tile counter as I stepped up onto the rattan barstool. "What's going on? Is everything all right?" I asked, and leaned over the counter as I took a bite of my salad.

Dad cleared his throat.

"It's your sister."

A discomfiting silence followed. I swallowed my food as a feeling of dread welled up inside.

Dad didn't call me often. He didn't have to. Since I had moved to Los Angeles almost six years earlier, I had a ritual of calling him once a week, usually on the weekends. But I had just spoken with him a few days earlier after Steve and I returned from our first vacation together. We had celebrated our one-year anniversary of the day we met with a ten-day romantic get-away to Jamaica. I was on edge because Dad's tone was the same tone I had heard when he called to let me know my sister-in-law had been killed in a car accident a few years back. It was also the same tone he had used six months ago when he told me my sister's boyfriend had left her and the kids.

I closed my eyes, took a long, deep breath and silently told myself, *Please God, let everything be okay*, before I asked, "What's going on?"

"Joan's in the hospital. She collapsed Friday at work and was taken by ambulance to the Brockton Hospital." Dad's voice was steady and clear. He tended to maintain a sense of calm and balance in a time of crisis. "It looks like she's had a stroke. Or at least that's what the doctors think at this time. She's partially paralyzed on the left side of her body."

"A stroke? Joan's had a stroke? But she's only twenty-nine! What do you mean she's had a stroke?" I pressed.

"I know, Laura. We're just as baffled about this as you are. We don't have a lot of answers right now." He breathed a long, heavy sigh. "I just came from the hospital. Her doctor said she might be there for some time, but we're not sure. They don't have a clear prognosis yet."

"Is she going to be okay? Where are the kids? Who's taking care of the kids?"

I slid down off the chair, walked into the living room, over to the sliding glass doors, peering onto the patio outside, searching for Steve. Unable to find him anywhere, I paced the room, gazing out the windows, while Dad explained what few details he knew.

My silence was finally broken when Dad said, "I hate to ask you this, but is there any chance you can come home and help us out? I don't know what to do here. It doesn't look very good."

My only sister Joan was a single mother raising three young children on her own. The two men who had fathered her three kids were absent from their lives; she was barely on speaking terms with them, if at all. She and I had never been the best of friends. Our distance had started early on in our youth. I hated my little sister "tagging" along behind me. By the time I reached my teenage years, I was clear she was an unwelcome guest in my presence. But our greatest dissonance came when I was eighteen, and she was fourteen, and she found out I had had an abortion. She took the Planned Parenthood pamphlets she found in my dresser drawer to Mom.

While I was sitting on my bed studying for a test one night, Mom came barging into our room. As she waved the abortion pamphlets in her hand, she screamed and hollered, "Did you have an abortion? Are you pregnant?" Mom had a tendency to be overly emotional and irrational when faced with difficult situations.

Though I lied and profusely denied the accusation, I felt deeply violated and betrayed by my sister.

Our distance lessened somewhat when Joan became a mother. I was genuinely happy for her. She loved being a mom and took great pride in her role. She doted over her kids. She hired clowns and ponies for their birthday parties, took them to the animal park regularly, and patiently read *each* of them their favorite bedtime stories every night. She found early on a way to share and express her love. I, on the other hand, would suffer fear and ambivalence toward motherhood for many, many years to come.

But now I was being called to go back home, to return to my family during a time of crisis. How could I refuse Dad's request? Though I was scheduled to leave for Maui the following week to attend a month-long art retreat, I couldn't picture myself basking in the tropics while Joan and her kids' lives were in a state of turmoil. So I rebooked my Hawaii ticket for a red-eye flight back home that night.

Steve didn't want me to go.

"I'm not sure it's a good idea, sweetheart. You know how troubling it is for you when you go back there," he said, stroking my hair as I lay in his arms moments before we left for the airport that evening.

"I know, but how can I say no? My family needs me. The kids need me," I replied, as tears dripped silently from the corners of my eyes.

"They can manage without you. You *can* say no," he urged.

Steve was a marriage and family therapist and knew only too well the pain and heartache I felt during and after my visits back East. Volatile outbursts often erupted between my mother and I, mostly prompted by her drinking. There were long-held resentments and hurts between the two of us. Mostly I didn't agree with her complaints and criticisms of my father. The way I saw it, she had become a bitter and scornful woman, and I tried my best to keep her at a healthy distance.

But I *had* to go back. I'd made a promise to be there, no matter what. Though I never thought anything would actually happen. Things like this only happened to *other* people.

The plane ride offered me time to be with my thoughts and memories, both good and bad. I knew things weren't all right. The signals had been there for some time. My sister was depressed over her recent breakup and had started drinking heavily. Dad told me she borrowed money from him more than once to pay her utility shut-off notices, and she didn't have gifts for her kids under the Christmas tree that year. I ignored the signs. I'd reached my limits. I tried to counsel her over the phone. I told her to stop drinking, go to AA, and get the support of a trained therapist to help her process the depression and loneliness she was feeling.

"Talk to Dad. He's been there. He knows the ropes better than anyone," is what I advised her.

"I know, I know," was all she said.

She never took my advice. Truth be told, I was annoyed she wouldn't clean up her life, the way I had mine.

I blankly stared out the airplane window into the black void of the night sky. My heart felt weighted and gloomy. I knew there was no one else to help pick up the pieces. It was impossible for me to imagine the full purpose and meaning of my return. Mostly I had the uneasy feeling my life was going to change in a monumental way. I felt a looming darkness; it was heavy, as if I were about to step into a deep, dark abyss.

# A Life Left Behind

A couple of years earlier, I had found myself in a rut. For over ten years I'd been obsessively focused on my professional career. Early on I knew my objective: I wanted to be somebody. In college, businessman icon Lee Iacocca caught my attention. I, too, wanted to be a savvy leader, empowering others through change and innovation. With an aptitude for numbers and a burning hunger for success, I entered the business world with my sights set on becoming a CEO.

I did everything necessary to get there. After graduating with a business degree, I entered the world of accounting and finance. When I wasn't on the job, I filled my waking hours staying up on current affairs by reading *Forbes*, *Newsweek*, and the *Wall Street Journal*. I stayed glued to informational television programs like *60 Minutes*, *20/20*, and *Primetime Live*. I was like a sponge sucking up everything I could learn in an attempt to move forward, to inch my way closer toward my goal.

Though I reached a level of professional recognition I had set out to accomplish, it had its price. My role as a financial controller for a real estate company began to feel orderly and dull. I felt as though something was missing in my life of spreadsheets and staff meetings. I was bored, unexcited by the day-to-day grind that had held my interest for years. Mostly, I felt empty and unfulfilled.

Shortly after my divorce, at the ripe age of thirty-one, I began seeing a psychotherapist. As I sat on Faye's beige couch week after week, sharing the intimate details of my life, trying to understand why I felt so unhappy and hollow, she offered some great advice. "Inquiry," she explained, "is a method used as a way of discovering deeper inner truth. And pondering helpful questions can, in time, lead one to understanding what motivates and inspires them."

So I began asking myself questions like *What am I doing with my life? What do I want? What's important to me?* The answers didn't come all at once; rather, they were revealed over time like a forgotten treasure waiting to be rediscovered.

Eventually I moved into an oceanfront townhouse with floor-to-ceiling windows and sounds of crashing waves that lullabied me to sleep nightly. I started every morning walking the deserted beach alone. It was a way for me to be in truthful conversation with who I was, to ask the questions, and to contemplate the focus and direction of my life. On those long solo walks along the shore, with my feet kicking the sand as the cool misty salt air slapped my face, I came to understand something about myself. I realized I had spent years working diligently to get to a place in my professional life I wasn't sure I wanted any longer. I began to wonder if I'd been following the wrong god all those years.

For the first time ever, I didn't know what I wanted. And to complicate matters, I wasn't sure what to do about it. I had *always* known what to do.

It was around that time when I met Steve. It was love at first sight. He was tall and handsome. His brilliant blue eyes gazed attentively upon me and cherishingly upon us. He was six years older than me, a wise, sensitive, native Californian who'd been a spiritual seeker most of his adult life. He called me his "Beloved" and possessed a talent for finding good in tough moments, seeing opportunities in the most imperfect of things.

Like the time he proposed to me on Christmas Day, when I was at my absolute worst. The flu came on Christmas Eve day, out of nowhere and took me down hard and fast. A chill ran through my body early in the morning as I stood at the kitchen counter sifting flour into a ceramic bowl, preparing for the upcoming festivities. By the end of the day, I was miserably laid out in bed with a stuffed nose, a raw scratchy throat, and a throbbing headache. A bottle of Nyquil sat on the nightstand while a hot water bottle rested under my pillow. During the night I had wrapped myself in three comforters trying to warm the chills and quivers from my body.

It was sometime during Christmas Day afternoon, when I appeared in the living room doorway, disheveled, my nose running, clinging to a box of Kleenex. Noticing my entrance, Steve rushed to my side, escorting me to the tan suede sofa next to the glistening Christmas tree.

While holding the box of Kleenex in my lap, I asked in a gruff voice, "Why are you here, all alone on Christmas Day?" Then I suddenly remembered it was his birthday. "Oh, my God, it's your birthday, Steve. Happy birthday! Why aren't you out celebrating with your friends?"

Elaborate plans had been made to celebrate Steve's fortieth birthday. George, Steve's best friend since early childhood, was throwing a birthday party with twenty of Steve's closest friends. We'd been planning it for months.

"My place is here with you, through sickness and in health," Steve said, his eyes moistened as he slipped his hand into his white cardigan pocket. He pulled out a small gold box with the tiniest red satin bow that sparkled in the glow of the Christmas tree lights. "I've been waiting all day to give this to you," he said, with the gift resting in the palm of his hand.

He reached for my hand, and like an offering, placed the box tenderly into my clammy palm. With my jaw hanging open, I looked at the box, then at him, then back at the box. Finally, I looked up into his gleaming eyes and said, "I thought we agreed not to give each other Christmas presents."

A month earlier, Steve had surprised me with a four-day trip to Maui for the long Thanksgiving Day weekend. We stayed at his friend Lori's house. While walking the beach and discussing our upcoming holiday plans, we agreed not to give each other material gifts that Christmas. Instead, we decided to gift one another an experience. My present to Steve for Christmas was a pair of tickets to a David Copperfield magic show.

"This is a special gift. A gift I've been fantasizing about giving you for some time now. It's my fortieth birthday gift from me to you, because of all the joy and love you bring into my life." He had tears in his eyes as a heartfelt smile spread across his face. Taking a breath, he moved his right hand over his heart, all the time nodding and smiling yes.

Staring at him wide-eyed and with a lump in my throat, I slowly opened the box. He knelt down and placed my hand into his. With a steady gaze, and tears in both our eyes, he placed a marquise diamond engagement ring on my finger, and proposed marriage.

Now you just gotta love a guy who has that kind of merit. I was crazy about him. Everything in me was a full "yes." Something opened inside me; an exalted love only poets speak of. Our union broke my silent longings. We gave ourselves to one another; our bodies were tied, our souls destined. My heart finally felt complete by the gift of being loved by him.

I had learned a different rhythm being with Steve. Since he

didn't see clients until 10 a.m., he started each morning waking up naturally. He rolled out of bed and began his day with a yoga and meditation routine, creating quiet time before his day took on speed. I, by contrast, had a long history of jumping out of bed to an alarm clock, hitting the pavement running usually by 6 a.m., moving at a fairly rapid pace, especially at work.

I was surprised one afternoon after I first moved to Los Angeles, when my new boss waved me into his office and said, "You'll get more with sugar than you will with salt." Apparently, one of my staff had complained I'd been too aggressive when I tossed a folder into her inbox saying, "I need a batch summary on my desk by 3:00 today," and walked away. She was upset, insulted that I had barked out commands rather than creating mutual rapport. My response to my boss was something like, "I told her what I needed. What's wrong with that?" He said I had great talents, but, "in California, we do things a little different." He recommended I use the word "please" in my approach. He told me I needed to slow down, connect with my staff, befriend and "play well" with them. "Help your team members find their greatness by cultivating a work environment that fuels them to be their best," he suggested.

I wasn't aware of the impact my drive to complete the task at hand had on others. At that time, I was much more interested in getting the job done, and not fully aware of the interpersonal skills I sometimes lacked. It would take me years to find the bridge between the two.

Steve helped me to understand that my stress and drive for success had consumed me. I had compromised myself, more than I wanted to admit, in search of something outside myself. In time, I made the decision to leave my job. I saved enough money to take a few months off, to rethink my career objectives. I wanted to use the time for deep inner reflection—to rediscover myself and my priorities.

A week before our trip to Jamaica, I moved into the Spanish ranch home Steve shared with his two housemates. Storage boxes were still stacked in the living room when I received the call from Dad. I was scheduled to leave for Maui the following week. Artist friends of Steve's had invited me to spend a month on the island, exploring art and the creative process as a way to decompress from the business world I had just left. I hoped the process of discovering the inner artist would help me uncover aspects about myself I knew lay dormant.

I was excited about the prospects that lay ahead. My identity of who I was and the roles I played were changing with the beginning of a new life with Steve, our future marriage, and the impending optimism of a more meaningful professional career. Life was full of possibilities. I could have easefully been born again, like a sunflower under a summer sun, standing in the garden, waiting to be anointed by heavenly rains.

This was the time of my life I had waited for, and finally arrived into.

# First Day On the Job

My flight arrived at Logan Airport at 6:45 the following damp, gray morning. Dad was waiting at the gate. His face was drawn, his eyes droopy. He looked old and tired standing in his Wrangler Jeans and short-sleeve pocket collar shirt, with a newspaper tucked under his folded arm. The gray in his hair was more noticeable since I had last seen him the summer before. We drove through the thick rush-hour traffic, straight to the Brockton Hospital. It was close to 9 a.m. when we arrived. Though visiting hours weren't until ten, we hoped to be allowed in for a brief visit.

Joan's room was diagonally across from the nurses' station. Dad walked up to the nurse in white scrubs standing at the counter, while I stood in the background watching him work his magic. He was a handsome, dark Irishman, a big guy with huge, strong work hands and beefy upper arms. With direct eye contact, he presented the facts for our early arrival in a concise manner and explained we needed to tend to Joan's children in the early afternoon, so we wouldn't be able to return later in the day.

He politely said, "We understand visiting hours aren't for another hour, but any break you can give us would be helpful." The nurse graciously permitted us a brief visit. Dad stayed behind talking with her a few moments as he motioned me with a nod of his head and a wave of his hand to go on ahead without him.

Joan was sitting upright in the bed staring at the wall-mounted TV screen. She was wearing a worn blue and white-striped hospital gown. Her auburn hair was in a long side braid hanging to the right of her face. Her right hand she held tightly in a fist. Her left hand lay lifeless on top of the white woven blanket.

Feeling awkward about her paralysis, I greeted her with a false smile, "Hey, Joan," as I walked over to the right side of the bed. I leaned over and gently kissed her on the cheek.

Though she jerked away, her eyes peered steadily up at the television screen. She didn't say a word to me. I stepped back and placed my purse on the corner of the bed near her feet. A strong sterile smell of lemon cleaning fluid permeated the air.

"What's wrong? You're not talking to me?" I asked.

She didn't utter a word, nor did she take her eyes off the TV. Perplexed by her lack of response, I sat down in the black vinyl and chrome chair, removed my purse from the bed, and placed it on top of my lap. I sat quietly, staring at her fixation with the morning news and commercials.

Moments later, Dad entered the room.

"Morning, Joan. How ya feeling, dear?" he asked, standing behind me with the *Boston Globe* in his hand.

She glazed over in his direction as she leaned her ear close to the TV, said an insincere "hello," and then turned her attention back toward the TV.

I looked up at Dad, slightly nodding my head in confusion. I shrugged my shoulders, looking to him for a clue. Befuddled, he returned the same gesture to me.

After some moments passed, I interrupted our silence when I said, "Joan, we only have a few minutes because we're here before visiting hours start. Dad's asked me to help out with the kids. Is there anything you want me to do? Anything I need to know?"

She didn't say a word.

Dad took a few steps toward her, leaned over the bed, and while lightly touching her right leg said, "Joan, Laura wants to know if you have any instructions for her with the children?"

Without taking her eyes off the TV, she replied, "No. I want to go home. I just wanna go home."

After Dad and I said our goodbyes, we walked out into the corridor, back over to the nurse's station. I was intent on finding some answers.

"The doctor's still gathering information. We're waiting for test results to come back," said the short, heavyset nurse from behind the counter.

"But she's not coherent. I've never seen her this way before. It's like she's not paying attention or doesn't comprehend what we're saying. Is she despondent? Is this common for stroke victims?" I peered at the nurse and then at Dad, who was standing behind me.

"Her doctor will be available to talk with you around eleven. I don't have any answers for you right now. I'm sorry," she replied.

"But, she didn't even respond when I talked about her kids. She loves her kids very much, but she didn't even respond. She's a single mom with three small children. Will she be able to take care of them?" I persisted anxiously.

"We don't have those answers right now. We're still trying to determine the type of stroke and prognosis. You need to talk directly with Dr. Price. He'll have more answers for you."

I prided myself on being capable of handling tough-call situations. Working in real estate sometimes presented emergency situations or even life-threatening circumstances such as heart attack victims, missing children, or violent family disputes. In a time of erratic behavior and crisis, for the most part, I kept a level head and was able to help others through difficult moments. But in this situation, I didn't have a clue how to work it.

Dad drove me to Joan's house. We sat in his Buick parked in the driveway as he gave instructions on what to do. He'd been managing everything on his own for the last two days and was exhausted. I saw his limitations that morning, something I hadn't seen much of before. He was a man's man, who, in my eyes, could be counted on for just about anything. He was charming and charismatic, yet down-to-earth and affable. He had his own moral compass and tried to do the right thing. I loved that he was fiercely loyal to his friends. I saw him more than once go into his wallet, pull out his last twenty, and hand it over to a friend or relative who was in need of a loan. People admired and looked up to him, sought him out for advice.

But that morning, sitting in his car, in the dead silence, both of us staring vacantly, trying to comprehend the recent tragic event, I knew he was depleted, clueless on how to manage the situation and move forward.

He handed me three hundred dollars in twenties, directions on the school and school bus schedule, and the telephone number of the neighbor's house where Lilly, Joan's youngest, had been since Friday evening.

"There's no food in the house. You'll find Joan's car keys on the fireplace mantel," he explained.

"Don't you want to come in?" I asked, hopeful. I didn't want to be alone.

With dark, tired eyes, he answered, "No, dear, I'm worn out. I've had all I can handle. I just want to go home and take a long nap. Thanks for your help. You have no idea what a godsend you are right now." He had a troubled look on his face. With a sigh, he reached his hand toward mine as he pulled me closer into him. He leaned over and kissed my forehead goodbye.

I was on my own.

A few years back, Dad had bought Joan and the kids a little fixer-upper. It was a thousand-square-foot dark brown saltbox with white shutters. Gosh, I think he only paid $60,000 for it. He wanted to help Joan and the kids out. He shared with me years earlier, after he and Mom separated, when he started revealing more of himself to me, "Maybe I was absent more than I should've been. I saw my role as the financial provider, that was all." He made up for his absenteeism over the years, to all of us, in different ways. For Joan it came by way of that house.

She had done a great job remodeling it over the years. Nothing structural, just small jobs like painting, wallpapering, and replacing light fixtures. She had recently laid a new black and white checkered ceramic tile bathroom floor.

When I walked into the house later that morning, it was a mess, with dirty dishes piled in the sink, newspapers tossed on the floor, and *Goosebumps* books and baseball cards cluttering the counters. Barbies and children's books were scattered everywhere, with dried, crusted, spilled dog food by the door. I started cleaning while waiting for the kids to make their way home from school.

Timmy and Tessy attended the same elementary school. Timmy was in second grade. He was a smart boy who early on was strong in his convictions, not easily persuadable. He wore a gold stud earring in his left ear and had had a hair tail most of his earlier childhood, a hairstyle he had recently outgrown. His mom called him the "man of the house," but he hated being the only male, with a mom and two sisters. "Even the dog is a girl," he had complained to me during my last visit the previous summer. Yet he took great pride in being the oldest, showing his younger sisters the ways of the world.

Tessy was tiny, with a thin wiry body weighing in at only forty-five pounds. She had long baby-fine blonde hair her mom often captured in artful ribbons, bows, and braids. She was a delicate, shy first grader, but in the presence of her family, she never held back. During my visits back East, I'd dress her up in frilly dresses and take her with me everywhere I went. I nicknamed her "Princess" because she was my treasured one. She had ignited a spark in my heart the day she was born. She brought out what was best in me and made me believe in myths, fairytales, and all things that were good in the world. The giant room within my heart was drenched by her innocence and beauty.

When the children arrived home from school, they were thrilled to see me, though they immediately wanted answers to questions I didn't have. We sat together on the kitchen porch steps, each of them leaning against my knees, facing one another, as I explained what little I could.

In a faint, humble voice, Tessy uttered, "But I miss my mommy, Auntie," and began to cry.

I pulled her in closer toward me.

"I want her to come home," she cried, as her little mouth quivered and puckered like a codfish.

"I want your mommy to come home too, Princess. The doctors are trying to help get her well." I leaned forward and kissed her watery eyes.

I wanted to bust out and cry myself, but I was afraid. I was afraid if they saw me crying they'd panic and become uncontrollably upset. So I held back. More than anything, I needed to be strong, to feel like I was in control, if not of the external circumstances, then at least with my own reactions and impulses.

Bowing her head low, Tessy whispered, "Is she going to die?"

Vigorously shaking my head, I quickly answered, "No, no, your mommy's not going to die." I tightly hugged them both.

Looking at me with adult worried eyes, Timmy asked, "Auntie, you're our Auntie and *my* godmother. You're gonna take care of us, aren't you?"

"Yes, Timmy, I'm here now, and I'm going to take care of you. So don't worry," I assured him, patting the top of his head.

An hour later, Dana, Lilly's babysitter, dropped off Lilly and Ruby, the family's cocker spaniel. Once she saw me, Lilly came running up the driveway with her stretched arms out wide, while Ruby leapt into Tessy's arms. Lilly was a cherub-like three-year-old with strawberry blonde hair, just like her mom's. My sister often referred to her as the "love baby," because she was the baby Joan had longed for when her two older children stopped being babies. Because I had moved to Los Angeles prior to her birth, I didn't have much of a relationship with her. We adored one another, though my yearly visits hadn't offered us an opportunity to form a bond the way I had with Timmy and Tessy.

Our first order of business was to fill the house with food. When we returned home from grocery shopping, still sitting in the back seat of the car, Timmy said, "Auntie, we'll take care of it from here."

"Take care of what?" I asked, preoccupied, reaching over into the back seat to unfasten Lilly's car seat, which she was trying to wiggle her way out of.

"We'll put the groceries away, Auntie. We do it all the time for Mom," Tessy answered assertively, unbuckling her seatbelt.

Together the two of them carried the brown paper bundles from the car into the house. Timmy lifted each bag, handing Tessy the lighter packages, while he carried the heavier ones. I stood watching them push chairs around the kitchen for each other. Tessy pulled the food out of the bags and passed them to Timmy as he stocked the cupboards, filled the pantry shelves, and packed the refrigerator. They completed the job by folding all the shopping bags. Tessy stacked the bags on the floor, and then Timmy placed them under the sink. I chuckled noticing how Joan mimicked mom's system of stacking grocery bags alongside the white plastic trash container.

It amazed and warmed my heart watching them work mutually together. They were only six and eight years old! It made me wonder how Joan had managed to organize a collaborative effort, which I sensed added to the success of her single-parent household.

The daylight quickly disappeared into darkness. We spent the remaining evening preparing, eating, and cleaning up after dinner. I did laundry, gave all the kids baths, and together we made lunches for school for the following day. By 9 p.m. everyone was tucked into bed, including me, as I collapsed, exhausted, into mine.

# Caretaking

The next few days revolved around meals, school, housekeeping, and caring for Lilly. Timmy was self-sufficient and a great help offering me instructions on the way things worked. He explained the protocol for early dawn trash removal, who certain people were who called looking for Joan, foods Lilly was allergic to, and in general, the regular routines Joan had created for her family.

Tessy, however, was a bit of an emotional challenge. Every morning after breakfast, she'd wander up to her room to get dressed for school. Although her clothing styles and choices were well matched and looked adorable on her, she thought otherwise.

"Oh, Princess, that's a wonderful outfit. Those white tights go great with your pink and white jumpsuit. You look beautiful," I said cheerfully, when she appeared at the bottom of the stairway one morning.

"No! I hate this. It looks *stupid*!" she screamed, as she yanked at her white blouse sleeve and tugged at the neckline. She stomped her foot several times, unbuckled the shiny pink belt, and threw it onto the floor. She clenched her hands into fists, pulled at her hair, turned around, and then trudged back up the stairway.

She responded the same way with every outfit she tried on.

Her breakdowns happened every day.

I'd then add fuel to her already out-of-control fury, by hollering up at her, "Tessy, you need to get it together before the school bus arrives."

Most mornings she left the house in tears, running like a crazed jackrabbit toward the bus. I was exhausted trying to get her out the door every morning, feeling like an incompetent, bad parent. In the early waking hours before the kids woke up, I lay in bed awake thinking and planning the day ahead. Since I was sleeping in the saggy twin spare bed in Tessy's room, I'd glance over at her sleeping soundly and cringe at the thought of her imminent breakdowns.

Lilly was with me most of the time and demanded my full attention. For the last several years during my visits back home, it had been common for me to take Timmy and Tessy out for an afternoon of fun and adventure. We'd spend the day at the zoo or Chuck E. Cheese, or once we took The T into the Boston Children's Museum, which we had to evacuate quickly because of a fire.

But playing the role of a parent, giving attention to a small child 24/7, wasn't something I had much experience with. I found myself putting Lilly in front of the TV with her Barbies and Ruby, the family's cocker spaniel, so I could take a shower or talk uninterrupted on the phone. I was ashamed when I realized how often I had judged friends, co-workers, even my sister, when they talked about setting their kids up in front of the tube. "Kids should be outdoors playing, not zombied out in front of a television set," I righteously added into conversations. Weren't we women bred to carry our babies on our hip, as we prepared dinner, while talking on the telephone, all at the same time? I criticized parents who allowed their children to watch TV based on their inability to manage it all simultaneously. Yet I found myself backpedaling when it was *I* who was in need of trying to manage it all. It didn't take long for me to find the TV to be my very own secret salvation.

During the hours Timmy and Tessy were in school, I spent the day tending to the care of the house, doing laundry, and running errands. But once the school bus dropped them off promptly at 2:50 everyday, I was on *their* time. Timmy had little league practice everyday after school from 4:00 to 5:00. And it wasn't an option for me to just drop him off and pick him up.

"But Mom and the girls *always* stay and watch my practice," he insisted, when I tried to convince him otherwise.

Joan had showed up for a long list of events in the kid's lives: baseball games, dance practice, school theatre productions, birthday parties, and little league bake sales. She had even encouraged Timmy and Tessy to set up a lemonade stand on their front lawn the previous summer. She cheered each of them on, supporting and encouraging them in whatever they did.

One late afternoon while sitting in the bleachers with the girls, a mother made the assumption Tessy and I were mother and daughter. The fact was we did look a little alike. We both had light color hair, thin body types, deep-set brown eyes, and a tiny nose. We even had the same scar on our lower chin and we both wore eyeglasses.

But Tessy didn't find her comment as endearing as I did. And she didn't waste a moment's breath correcting the mistaken mother. She stood up straight, erect like a military officer, with her arms stiff by her side and her hands tightly balled. Her eyes went feral as she placed both her hands on her hips and said in an insistent manner, "She's not my mother! She's my Auntie! *My* mother's in the hospital!"

Even though the mother profusely apologized, Tessy spent the remaining hour under the bleachers in a foul mood.

Although Timmy was a well-behaved boy and mostly

listened to me, he had his moments. When it came time to go to Tessy's weekly dance class, he was vocal with his resistance.

"But I don't wanna hang around a bunch of *girls* dancing. It's not fair," he griped, slumped in the back seat of the car with both arms folded around his backpack, which he tucked in close to his chest.

Before I had a chance to respond, Tessy, who was sitting in the front seat, turned around to him and said, "Yeah, well, if we have to go to your *stupid* baseball practice, you can at least come to my dance practice."

It wasn't long before they were arguing with one another, each pleading for me to aid in their defense. I hadn't seen much rivalry between them over the years. Sure they argued; all siblings do. But as the days without their mother continued to mount, so too did their struggles with one another.

I only saw Joan once more over those first few days. I didn't want to visit her. I was angry she didn't appreciate my service to her and her family in their time of need. Mostly I didn't want to go back to the hospital because of the growing tension between us.

While sitting with her in her hospital room, I said to her, "Oh, yeah, I had to run to the mall yesterday to buy Timmy some white tube socks with red stripes for his upcoming game this Saturday."

She didn't respond, but I could see her seething as she clenched her jaw and tightened her right fist.

Then I continued with, "Yesterday morning, Tessy left the house without her lunchbox. So Lilly and I stopped by her school to drop it off and we met her teacher, Mrs. Hartman."

Again, Joan didn't have anything to say, though she grabbed the remote control and turned the volume up on the TV.

As I stood up to leave, I said, "By the way, Lilly asked me

to give these cookies to you. We baked them this morning for Timmy's field trip to the dairy farm tomorrow." I pulled a small plastic baggie of cookies out of my purse and placed it on the side table.

With her right hand, shaky as it was, Joan pulled out a Marlboro cigarette box from under the white woven blanket. She drew a cigarette from the pack, placed it in her mouth, and lit it.

I shook my head sneeringly and said through clenched teeth, "Joan, this is a hospital. Smoking is *not* allowed."

She turned her head toward me, blew smoke my way, and then turned her head back toward the TV.

Fuming, I said sharply, "Joan! This is a hospital. You're not allowed to smoke. It's against the law."

She gave me a piercing glance and said, "I don't fucking care. And *don't* tell me what to do."

Furious and unable to influence her actions, as I once had been able to do, I took a step back. Her disposition rattled, even scared me. Being the older one, I once had power over my little sister. Actually, I bossed her around quite a bit when we were kids. She looked up to me, was even envious of my life—my marriage to my long-term boyfriend, a successful career, my move to Los Angeles. We had both witnessed each other's mean streak in our younger years. But I'd never seen her vicious or hostile toward me the way I witnessed her that day.

In the evenings, after I put the kids into bed, it was my time to be with Steve. Most nights Tessy quickly fell fast asleep and it didn't wake her when I talked with Steve while lying in my bed in her room. Because of the time zone difference, Steve arranged his schedule to be available for us to talk every night at nine. He was my only escape from the intensity of the world that engulfed me. He was what I looked forward to most in my day. Since Steve was a therapist, he offered valuable insights into behaviors I didn't quite understand.

"Timmy and Tessy's fighting is most likely a reaction to them being separated from their mother," he explained.

"I'm worn out. I've only been here five days, but it feels like an eternity," I said, slumped on my bed, with the cordless phone propped up to my ear by a pillow.

"Have you seen or talked with your mother yet?" he asked.

"No, not yet. Dad told me he called her as soon as he received word about Joan being hospitalized. He said she told him she was too busy working and couldn't take time off to help out."

"Oh, really?" he replied.

"Yeah. I'm surprised she hasn't called the kids. I'm not sure what to make of it."

"Has she been to the hospital to see Joan?"

"I don't know. I'm sure Dad would've told me if she had. He's been there everyday."

"Do you have any idea why she wouldn't visit her daughter?"

"I don't know. When I was in the hospital a couple of years ago, I didn't hear from her either. Not even flowers or a phone call."

"Wow, she really is unavailable," he said.

"Yeah."

"Well, I miss you very much, sweetheart," he said.

"I miss you too."

My sleepy eyes welled with tears as I peered out the window into the dark night. My *real* life felt so far away.

"When are you coming home?" Steve asked.

"Soon I hope. Soon."

# The Release

While vacuuming the oval chestnut braided rug in the living room the following Monday morning, the telephone rang. Dad was on the other end.

"Joan just called me from the hospital. She wants me to come by after school and pick her up. She says she's being released."

"What? What do you mean she's being released? Have you talked to her doctor?" I asked.

"No. Why do I need to talk with her doctor?" He let out a long exhale that fell between an impatient sigh and a groan.

"Just like that, she's being released? You told me last week her doctor said most likely after her hospital stay she'd go into a rehab program for her paralysis." Before Dad had a chance to speak, I jumped in and added, "Have they figured out what's wrong with her? You told me yesterday the doctors still didn't know the cause of her stroke. Did they find out?" I was pacing the kitchen floor while wrapping the telephone cord tightly around my fingers.

"I don't know, Laura. What do you want me to do? What am I supposed to do here?" he replied. What followed next was a long, heavy moan.

I could picture his furrowed brow in my mind.

"Dad, she's been in the hospital for ten days. Last I heard

she's still partially paralyzed. I don't understand why they would release her. Did you visit her yesterday?"

"Yes."

"Well, how was she?"

"The same."

There was a pause.

"You know, more than anything I want her to be back home with her family. God knows I want to be back home in California. But something isn't right. I don't know what it is, but something's just not right." I was eyeing the collage of family photo magnets Joan proudly displayed on her refrigerator. She'd been collecting them for years. It was all there: each of the kids as babies and toddlers in their Halloween costumes at the pumpkin patch. Every birthday celebration was framed, along with school pictures, and Timmy in his baseball uniform and Tessy in her dance outfits.

My trance was interrupted, when Dad said, "I don't know, Laura. I just don't know any more."

There was another pause.

"Well, what did you tell her?" I asked.

"I told her I'll be out of school by 11:45. I thought you might want to come along, so I said I'd be there around one o'clock."

Dad had been a Boston high school English teacher for more than thirty years. Ever since I could remember, he was out the door by 5:40 every morning. He was punctual and dependable. Since it was now June, and finals were held in the morning, he was most often out of school before noontime.

We arrived at the hospital a few minutes before one. We walked over to the nurse's station. There were three nurses, all dressed in slate blue scrubs, talking to one another behind the counter.

Just as I was about to interrupt them, Dad gently tapped my shoulder. Dr. Price, Joan's doctor, was approaching the nurse's station. He immediately recognized Dad and extended his bulky right hand toward him.

"Hello, Mr. Maher," he said.

"Hello, Dr. Price," Dad replied, as they shook hands.

"This is my daughter, Laura, Joan's older sister." Dad took a step back, allowing the doctor to offer me an unobstructed handshake.

Dr. Price was an older gray-haired man, standing almost six-four with a tanned weathered face, like a seasoned seaman. He had bushy white eyebrows and an enormous white moustache.

"Nice to meet you," he said, shaking my hand.

"We're here to pick up Joan," said Dad.

"Ah, yes," he replied, nodding his head.

"I'm curious to know why you're releasing her?" I asked.

"Sure, I'll be happy to talk with you and answer your questions. Why don't you both follow me, so we can speak privately." With a wave of his hand, he gestured us down the corridor. We followed him past several rooms, down the brightly lit hallway, into a small blue-carpeted room with a well-worn black desk. As he took his seat behind the desk, he motioned for Dad and I to sit in the two black vinyl and chrome chairs opposite him.

I didn't waste a moment's time starting the conversation. "I don't understand why Joan's being released. Apparently you told Dad last week that most likely Joan would be going into rehab for her paralysis. Has that changed?"

He leaned forward and placed his interlocked fingers on top of the desk. "Most stroke patients *do* go on to rehabilitation. But Joan," he said, as he shook his head, then pursed his lips, "is very clear she doesn't want any help from us."

I too leaned forward, resting my arms on my purse in my lap. "What do you mean?"

"She's been resisting us since she arrived. She's not following hospital regulations by smoking in the room, and although she's been told it's not permitted, she doesn't listen. She's disrupting the patient who shares a room with her by smoking and watching TV late at night. She's uncooperative, even hostile toward the nurses, making unreasonable demands. She's very insistent that she be released." He lowered his head, and then looked back up at us and continued, "The truth is, she's a very difficult patient and more important, we can't keep her here against her will." He relaxed back into his chair.

"I notice she's either non-responsive or angry, even hostile like you said. I've never seen her that way before. Is this common for stroke victims?" I asked.

"Some patients do become withdrawn. I don't know why she's angry. That could be psychological."

"Have you found out what type of stroke she's had? Or what caused it?" I asked.

"No." He looked over at Dad. "As you and I have previously discussed, Mr. Maher, we're sure she's had a stroke. But we're unclear of anything more than that at this point in time. We're still running tests. But, this *is* unusual."

"How so?" I asked. Worried, I looked over at Dad.

"She's so young. We usually don't see stroke victims her age."

There was a troubling silence in the room.

The doctor briefly sniffed the air while twisting the tip of his mustache and said, "We just don't know. I wish I had more to tell you, but I just don't know. I'm sorry."

I slumped back into my chair feeling defeated, when the kids came to mind.

"Is she well enough to take care of her children? She's a

single mother with three young kids. Is she well enough to take care of them?"

"I don't know," he said faintly, as his shoulders rose, then collapsed. "I just don't know."

Before we left the office, Dr. Price pulled out a prescription pad from his white jacket pocket. He leaned over the desk and jotted down the name and number of a local outpatient doctor who he thought might be of further help to us.

As he handed me the paper, he said, "The best thing you can do for Joan right now, is to keep her stress level down and pay close attention to her behaviors."

# Something's Wrong

On the silent drive back to Joan's house, I sat in the back seat looking out the window, hoping and praying Joan would return to her life, and everything would be all right. We picked up Lilly, who was with the babysitter, and made it home just in time for the school bus drop off. Joan hid behind the kitchen door. When Timmy and Tessy entered the kitchen, Joan popped out from behind the door yelling, "Surprise!"

"Mommy, you're home!" Tessy cried out in elation, dropping her backpack, flinging her arms wide open, leaping into Joan's arms. With her left arm motionless by her side, Joan hugged Tessy tightly with her right arm, as they dropped to the floor laughing.

"I missed you so much, Mommy," said Timmy, as he gently hopped onto his mother's back, squeezing her from behind.

Hearing the commotion, Lilly, who was sitting in the living room watching TV, came running into the kitchen with her doll in tote. She threw her hands high up into the air and shouted, "Yeah!" before joining in on the fun. They were all frolicking on the blue speckled linoleum floor like a pod of great whales in the sea.

Tessy didn't leave her mommy's side for the remainder of the day. She sat pleased and contented by Joan's feet on the living room rug in front of the fireplace, coloring happy, smiling pictures of her family. Dad and Timmy went to the store and bought a welcome home cake. I made pasta for dinner, and we sat around the kitchen table laughing and talking like any other normal day.

After Dad left, we huddled on the couch and watched a movie together. The tightness and tension dissipated as my body began to relax. All seemed well in our world again. I felt the beginning of an easing for us all. Everyone went to bed happy and full of good cheer.

The following afternoon while I was in the kitchen clearing out the dishwasher, Joan walked in, poured herself a cup of coffee and said, "I can manage it on my own now."

"What do you mean?" I asked, turning toward her too quickly. I lost hold of a plate, but caught it before it hit the floor.

"I'm back home and can take care of my family by myself. So you can leave now," she replied, before she turned around and walked out of the room.

I stood motionless in the kitchen, not quite believing what I had just heard. *How could she possibly think she's ready to fully resume her life?* I wondered if Joan was aware of the possible impact the stroke could have on her and her family. Even though she had regained some movement in her body, she still didn't have feeling and control of her left arm and hand.

I wanted more than anything to be back home in California with Steve. Though he and I continued to talk on the phone nightly, I missed being in his arms. It was the first time since Steve and I met that we had been separated for more than a few days from one another. I yearned for our long, romantic arm-in-arm moonlit walks on the beach, where we talked about the happenings of our day. I missed curling up on the sofa with my head resting on his lap, sipping tea, and reading books together. I missed my white cat, Winter, and the way she burrowed her head under my chin. I longed for my daily hikes and weekly visits to the farmer's market. I pined for the cozy comforts of home and someone looking out for me. I was tired, stressed, and worn out from caring for my sister's family.

But I wasn't convinced it was time for me to leave yet.

I followed Joan into the living room. "Hey, Joan, it's great you're back home. But I think it's important for me to hang out for a few more days, just to make sure everything goes smoothly."

"Why? I'm fine," she replied, sitting back on the brown plaid sofa, sipping coffee.

"The doctor said it's crucial you keep your stress level down so you don't end up having another stroke," I said, as I picked the Barbies up off the floor and placed them into the pink plastic carry case. "I can help out by cooking and driving Timmy to and from baseball practice, since the doctor has advised you not to drive. You're also on medication, and you don't have full mobility of your body yet. I think you should take advantage of me being around a few days longer to help you get back into the swing of your life again."

She didn't really agree with the way I saw things, but went along with it. Well, she didn't actually go along with it either; it was more like she didn't argue the point. Instead, she stood up, and while holding the white ceramic coffee mug with the image of her and the kids at Santa's Village two Christmases ago, she walked out of the room, away from me and the conversation.

I spent the following days trying to stay in the background as best I could. Joan parented her children while I helped out with the mundane tasks of laundry, food shopping, and preparing meals. I took her to a couple of local doctors. She didn't want to go, but I insisted, because something still wasn't right. I couldn't put my finger on it or name it. It was a feeling, nothing more. She was absent in conversations. She didn't always respond when the kids or I asked her questions. She had a vacant look on her face, and her eyes were glazed when watching TV. Or she'd stare out into space for long periods of time while sitting at the kitchen table drinking coffee.

Unfortunately the doctors didn't have any answers for us either.

The following Saturday morning, I slept in because it was a non-school day, and I wanted to give Joan time to enjoy a meal with her kids without me around. When I walked into the living room, sometime around 8:30, I found all three kids huddled in front of the TV in their pajamas watching cartoons. They were eating Reese's Peanut Butter Cups from a plastic bag. There was a huge pile of unwrapped orange foil wrappers in the center between them.

"Timmy, have you guys had breakfast yet?" I asked, as I tightened the belt across my robe.

"We *are* Auntie. Mom let us have candy for breakfast. She's the *best* Mom," he said cheerfully, with chocolate smeared all over his lips.

Joan took great pride in feeding her family a hearty meal every morning. She mimicked Mom in that way, valuing the importance of starting the day off with a substantial breakfast, "fuel for the day," as Mom used to say. Most weekends she cooked her special French toast recipe. So I was surprised seeing the kids eat candy so early in the morning.

I walked into the kitchen. The windows were open, and the fresh warm morning air filled the room. Joan sat at the round oak kitchen table drinking a cup of coffee and reading the newspaper.

"Morning, Sis. How'd you sleep?" I asked, as I opened the refrigerator door. I pulled out a carton of orange juice.

"Morning," she mumbled, without taking her eyes away from the newspaper.

"Hey, what's up with the kids eating candy for breakfast?" I asked, as I pulled a glass from the cabinet.

"What's wrong with *that*?" she responded, still holding the newspaper.

My body froze as I stood at the counter with the carton of OJ in one hand and an empty glass in the other. I wondered, *What's she thinking? Does she really believe it's okay to give the kids candy for breakfast?*

While parenting her kids, Joan had learned the skill of picking and choosing her battles. She had explained to me, both in words and in actions, how one never wins them all, the importance of children winning some, and how to choose those battles that will make a lasting positive impact. I decided not to argue the point about the kids eating candy, but made a mental note of it.

The following day I was in the kitchen making tuna fish sandwiches for everyone. I heard the sound of water running in the bathroom. After filling the bathtub, Joan placed Lilly into the tub, walked into the kitchen, poured another cup of coffee, then walked out into the living room, and sat in front of the TV.

Moments later I stepped into the living room. "Joan, can I finish giving Lilly a bath for you?" I asked, drying my hands on a dishtowel.

Without looking away from the TV, she replied, "I've got it covered."

I waited for her to get up and tend to her daughter's bath. But she didn't make a move. Eventually I turned around and walked back into the kitchen, uncertain what to do. An uneasy feeling welled up from inside. *Is a three-year-old okay in a bathtub on her own?* I stood in the kitchen immobilized, feeling torn. I didn't know what to do.

Finally, I had an idea. I walked over to the bathroom door, knocking loud enough for Joan to hear from the other room. I announced to Lilly, and Joan, "I need to go to the bathroom Lilly, and I'm coming in."

When I opened the door, I caught Lilly sitting on the edge of the white porcelain pedestal vanity. The mirrored medicine cabinet was open wide. She was painting her fingernails, or fingers actually, with red metallic nail polish. That wasn't so much of a big deal. What really scared me was when Lilly tried hiding the evidence by putting her freshly painted fingers into her mouth. My heart raced as I lunged at her, pulling her fingers out of her mouth. I examined her, as well as the contents of the cabinet to see if there was anything else she had gotten into. I cleaned her up, bathed and dressed her, and together we walked out into the living room.

Joan was still sitting on the sofa watching TV. With Lilly's hand in mine, I walked her over to the sofa, stood in front of Joan and said, "I walked into the bathroom and found Lilly painting her fingers with nail polish. She tried hiding it from me by sticking her hands in her mouth. Do you know that ingesting nail polish is toxic and can be fatal?" I reached down and turned both of Lilly's hands over so Joan could see the nail polish stains.

Joan reached over the maple coffee table, grabbed a cigarette, and then lit it.

In a loud voice, I asked, "Joan, do you hear me?"

She stood up and eyed me coldly as she exhaled a cloud of smoke. She waved the freshly lit cigarette in her right hand and shouted at me. "You're not welcome here anymore! I want you out! I want my life back. I don't want you telling me or my kids what to do anymore."

Placing my hands on my hips, I replied, "I'm just trying to help. Something's not right here. I'm sorry, but you're sick. You don't see it, but I do. Something's very wrong here." I tried to stay calm, but I felt the edge of my boiling point, as I too was at my end.

Narrowing her eyes like a cornered cat, she said, "It's just like when we were kids. You were always bossing me around. Well, this is *my* house and I'm not gonna let you boss me or *my* kids around anymore." She took an inhale from her cigarette, walked over toward me, stood in front of my face, and then blew cigarette smoke into my eyes.

Fuming and protecting my position, I pulled out my bitch card and yelled right back into her face with my arms clenched into fists by my side. "I didn't volunteer for this job; this wasn't my idea! I'm not here for you; I'm here for your kids! You're being an ungrateful bitch, and I'm sick of it!"

Just then Lilly let out a scream and began to cry. We had forgotten she was in the room with us. Joan and I looked cross-eyed at each other, but didn't say another word. Joan walked over toward Lilly, picked her up with her right arm, and as she turned her back away from me, she said, "Your Auntie's a fucking bitch."

I turned around, stormed out of the room, through the kitchen, out the side door, into the heat of the sun, livid with rage. My heart was pounding hard and fast. Pacing in the back yard, with the sun beating down on me, I began to make a list of all the reasons I was right, and she was wrong. Thoughts of taking flight, getting on a plane and abandoning my sister raced through my mind. I wanted more than anything to disappear, to run off and leave her alone fending for herself.

But I didn't leave. The sound of Tessy's ringing bicycle bell in the front driveway brought me out of my rage. I remembered the kids and my promise to be there for them, to take care of them. I didn't leave because I knew that in dire moments, no matter how dreadful things may appear, there's always a moment of ease, or grace, or something that makes everything that happened before seem so inconsequential. What mattered more than my anger, more than my rage, more than the contempt I felt toward my sister, was my desire not to run away, as I had so many times before.

# The Prognosis

The skies were stormy, and the city traffic was heavy and noisy as Joan and I made our way into Boston. The flapping windshield wipers echoed as we drove in heavy silence. I had found a doctor at Brigham and Women's Hospital who specialized in strokes in young adults. Surprisingly, we were able to get an appointment the very next day. I dragged Joan reluctantly to the appointment, promising her it was our last doctor's visit. And it was the last one because I had completely run out of options. I had nowhere else to turn and banked everything on this visit, hoping we would find some answers.

Dr. Gordon was a man in his early forties, with a crew cut and handsome jade-green eyes. His spacious office was creamy yellow, with track lighting that was easy on the eyes. His large double-pedestal cherry wood desk held half a dozen pictures of his family grouped together in the right corner. He sat behind the desk in a large black leather swivel chair, mulling through Joan's medical records and recent test results I had picked up the day before from the Brockton Hospital. Joan and I sat opposite him in comfortable soft blue leather wingback chairs.

After he examined Joan, he asked her questions, such as *What does a typical day look like? How is your ability to stay focused? What tasks are more difficult since the stroke?* After

Joan responded to each question, I offered my own answers, oftentimes different than what she said—for example, when Dr. Gordon asked her if she was able to get up every morning and feed the children breakfast.

She told him nonchalantly, "Sure, not a problem," and left it at that.

I looked at the doctor and cleared my throat.

Looking over at me, he asked, "Do you have anything to add?"

"Yes," I replied. "Last weekend Joan fed her kids Reese's Peanut Butter Cups for breakfast. When I asked her why, she replied, 'What's wrong with that?'"

Joan didn't question or defend my response. She just turned her head in the opposite direction, away from the doctor and I. I knew she didn't like hearing me say things contrary to her, but I believed we were at a critical time in finding answers *I* desperately wanted. I wasn't about to lie for her.

Dr. Gordon continued asking questions, as his gold pen moved swiftly across the paper. Eventually I explained to him, in great detail, the recent bathing incident with Lilly.

After gathering all the available data, Dr. Gordon placed his pen on his desk, and reclined backwards in his chair, folding his arms behind his head. He took a deep breath, leaned in closer, placed his hands on top of the desk, and said, "All evidence supports you've suffered from a frontal lobe stroke." He went on to explain the frontal lobe of the brain is involved in planning, organizing, problem solving, and selective attention. "The portion known as the prefrontal cortex controls personality and various higher cognitive functions such as behaviors and emotions. A stroke often results in an inability to perform tasks that are complex or require sequential steps to complete, such as preparing a meal, dressing oneself, or grocery shopping," he said. He then continued, "In basic terms, the stroke has affected your decision-making process."

Joan didn't react. She didn't mutter a word or ask any questions. She sat in her chair with her hands resting in her lap, wearing a drawn, empty look on her face.

"How did this happen? We don't have a history of strokes in our family," I asked, leaning forward on the edge of my chair with a pen and pad of paper in my hands. I continued taking notes as he further explained.

"Joan's been under a tremendous amount of stress since a recent breakup. It sounds like she's been trying to manage a lot on her own. My guess is, it's a combination of stress, alcohol, three to fours hours sleep a night for the last six months, plus drinking fifteen cups of coffee a day, in an attempt to keep it all going." He picked up his gold pen and placed it in the round leather penholder.

"Fifteen cups of coffee a day?" I turned to my sister, shaking my head in doubt, silently questioning her as to the accuracy of his statement.

She didn't utter a word, but gave me a curt nod that told me to *back off.*

I turned back to the doctor and said, "She's drinking that much coffee?"

"Apparently so," he replied, nodding his head yes, looking toward her for validation.

I myself have never been a coffee drinker. I knew Joan loved coffee, but I didn't really notice anything unusual. Sure, I saw her grab a cup of coffee several times a day at home. Plus twice a day she walked down to Dunkin' Donuts, which was only a few blocks from her house, to grab coffee after the kids left for school and before they returned home. I thought her reason for leaving the house was to take a break from me, from us.

Dr. Gordon's prognosis was clear and succinct. "The help

and attention you receive within the next year will more or less determine how you'll be for the remainder of your life. This next year is critical," he said, and then added as he looked at me, "She needs to relearn cognitive skills lost due to the stroke."

He suggested we find a cognitive care facility, a full-time treatment center that would offer Joan the tools needed to relearn basic life skills she'd lost. He gave Joan a list of don'ts.

"You shouldn't drink any more coffee and definitely not a drop of alcohol. And you're not allowed to drive a vehicle either," he advised. Then he dropped the bomb. "I'm sorry to have to tell you, but I don't believe you're capable of taking care of your children."

I was stunned into silence. My mouth went dry, as a chill ran through my body. I looked over at Joan. She remained emotionless, sitting in the chair with her hands still folded on her lap. The only way I knew she heard what the doctor had said was the now familiar visible sign when she took her gaze away from him and stared vacantly out into space.

We staggered out of his office into the long hollow corridor. We walked in silence as Joan's sneakers squeaked against the floor a few steps behind me. I felt weak, jelly-like in my body. I didn't know what to say to Joan for the longest time. I only knew our recent findings presented another dismal cloud of gloom ahead of us.

Outside, the streets were wet with rain. As we walked back to the parking garage, I started to say something.

Joan abruptly cut me off saying, "If you say anything to me, I'll fucking punch the hell out of you. And if you don't believe me, just try me. Just fucking try me."

I'd never been afraid of my younger sister. I knew she was

physically bigger and tougher than me, but I could out-bitch her, making her back way off. We'd never ever hit or touched one another, or been abusive in any way other than words. But I had a chilling thought she just might rip me to shreds, so I kept my mouth shut the entire ride home.

# Childhood Trauma

Life with my sister and her family became quite the daunting wild ride. Joan and I were constantly at each other's throats and didn't have a kind word to say to one another. We weren't just bickering; we were in each other's way, all the time. She complained I used her car much more than was necessary, while I protested every cigarette she smoked. Every day I sat at the kitchen table with the telephone book in front of me, talking with different agencies, trying to find a program for her. Joan resisted my trying to get her the help she needed. She didn't want me organizing her life. She didn't want to go anywhere, except back to the life she had before *I took it over*.

I knew she was ill, not in her right mind, but I couldn't let her into my heart. My body was in a continual state of contraction and rigidity. I resented the role I was playing. The way I saw it, I was the one cleaning up after her mess. I was livid she wasn't appreciative of what I was doing for her. In my mind, I silently kept track and recounted all her shortcomings.

Steve tried to help me understand the bigger picture.

"Your family's in a crisis, sweetheart," he said late one evening over the phone. "Your sister has had a stressful physical and emotional event, which is causing traumatic change in her and her kid's lives. Unfortunately, it sounds like she's in denial and unable to cope with the reality of it all."

"So what do I do?" I asked, exhausted, almost pleading.

"You need to guide her and her family through this difficult time. The upside is that it can be a tremendous opportunity for growth, for all of you. You know oftentimes difficult events in one's life are a disguise for opportunities for growth and transformation."

*Growth? Transformation?* I could only focus on the current situation at hand. I couldn't sleep. I couldn't eat. I couldn't find the time to take a daily walk. I was frustrated, stressed, boiling with rage. And I blamed my sister for every seething ounce of violence burning inside me.

One day after school, Tessy walked into the living room while I sat on the sofa folding clothes. She carried two naked Barbie dolls in one hand and her rectangular plastic pink Barbie carry case in the other.

"Auntie, will you play Barbies with me?" she asked, nestling the Barbies close to her chest.

"I can't right now, Tessy. I'm folding clothes."

*"Please. Pretty please,"* she begged, squeezing the Barbies tighter.

"I can't, Tessy!" I shouted. "I have laundry to fold. Then I need to take Timmy to his practice. Then I need to go to the grocery store and pick up something for dinner tonight. Then I need to make dinner." The whole time I ranted I stayed focused on folding the clothes.

Her pleading gave way to a disappointing frown. She dropped the Barbies and the carry case where she stood. Tears filled her brown eyes as she hung her head low, turned around, and walked out of the room.

I didn't stop or go after her. I stayed on the sofa folding the clothes. In her moment of need, I wasn't available for her.

More than anything I wanted to lie down on the floor beside my Princess and pretend our lives were perfect and happy. But in that moment, I believed my *to do* list needed more attention than her. I felt as if I were a brittle sliver of glass ready to shatter into a billion pieces. I could hardly remember what it felt like to smile at a sunset or laugh at a funny movie. And to make matters worse, I felt gravely disappointed I wasn't able to attend Katherine and Dennis's wedding with Steve back home in California.

It was the first wedding Steve and I would have attended as a couple. Steve and Dennis were long-time friends, and Steve was an usher in the wedding. The ceremony was at Lake Shrine, a sanctuary in Pacific Palisades Steve and I were contemplating using for our own wedding. I had bought a gorgeous strapless ivory lace dress for the occasion. We had both looked forward to the celebration, and I felt a huge sadness not attending the wedding with Steve. I wanted to break down and cry right then and there, when Tessy walked out of the room in tears. But I couldn't. *Things* had to get done. I *had* to keep going. I *had* to keep it together. I wasn't surprised when moments later, I broke up a spat between Tessy and Timmy.

I'd never experienced a state of depression in my life. I'd never been able to relate when others shared their battles in trying to find a ray of light in their despairing, hopeless lives. But I felt disheartened, deflated in every way possible being with my sister and her crisis. I didn't know how I was keeping it all together. I was stressed out, my sister and I were fighting all the time, and I didn't see an end in sight. I seriously needed a break from it all.

Help arrived when Sherry, Timmy and Tessy's aunt on their dad's side, called early one Thursday evening. She offered to come by and take the kids the following Saturday afternoon.

Sherry was a sprightly thirty-something-year-old schoolteacher who didn't have children of her own. Even though the kids didn't have any contact with their dad, Sherry was in their life. She attended their birthday parties, stopped by with holiday gifts, and occasionally took the kids for an afternoon outing to the park or a matinee. What really impressed me was whenever she took the kids or delivered gifts, she always included Lilly, even though Lilly wasn't her biological niece. She was kindhearted that way.

After Sherry gathered the kids on Saturday, I escaped to Dad's apartment for the afternoon. When I arrived back at Joan's house, shortly before 6 p.m., the kids were eagerly awaiting my arrival.

"Auntie, Auntie, Mommy's drunk. She's passed out on the sofa," yelled Timmy, sprinting toward the door, greeting me as I reached for the aluminum screen door handle.

"Yeah, we thought our mommy was dead," said Tessy, leaning against Timmy, reaching for my hand.

"Huh? What's going on?" I gulped. I felt cold with panic as I entered the house. Picking up Tessy's still trembling body, I laid her head on my shoulder while looking around for Sherry.

Sherry stood in the living room doorway, in the background, not saying a word. She didn't have to—the kids pretty much said it all.

"Yeah, Auntie, we came home from the park a little while ago and found mom lying on the floor," Timmy narrated, pointing to the spot on the living room rug where they had found her. "We thought she was dead. We thought our mommy was dead."

Lifting her head off my shoulder, Tessy whimpered, "I was screaming and crying, yelling for her not to die, Auntie. I didn't want my mommy to die."

"Aunt Sherry yelled for me to dial 911, while she tried helping Mom," Timmy gasped. "And just after I dialed 911, then Aunt Sherry told me to hang up. She told me to hang up because she said Mommy was just drunk and passed out."

Tessy picked her head up off my shoulder again and looking at me with bug eyes, said, "Yeah, she wasn't dead at all, Auntie. Mommy was drunk, not dead."

Later that evening I called Steve, but he didn't answer, so I called my girlfriend Shirley in Los Angeles. She was ten years older than me and had had a similar experience years ago when her younger sister, a single mom, had become sick and was unable to care for her only child. Shirley had stepped in, acting as parent to her niece for a period of time. Shirley knew, even better than I, the role I was trying to play. While lying in my bed, I shared with her the latest episode, hoping to get some support from her.

"Sounds like your sister's trying to numb her pain as a way to cope with the situation," she said.

"Maybe so, but the doctor was very clear she shouldn't drink alcohol. And she's still drinking coffee. It's like she doesn't care. She hates it when I say anything to her about it."

"Sounds like you're pretty upset with her."

"Well, yeah. She's trying to manage her problems by drinking, just like the way our mother did. I moved to L.A. to get away from all this dysfunction," I countered.

"Where's your compassion? Your sister's ill right now; she can't help herself."

"Compassion? You're kidding me, right? She shouldn't have had kids if she can't take care of them, or herself for that matter. She's a mess, and I resent cleaning up after her."

# The Threat

A nd things got even worse.
   One day while the kids were at school, and Lilly was sitting in front of the TV twisting the string on her animal cracker box with Ruby by her side, I thought it would be a good time to run an errand. Joan was sitting on the sofa smoking a cigarette while reading the newspaper. I walked over to the fireplace, grabbed the car keys from the mantel, and announced, "I'll be back in less than an hour. I'm going to the mall to run an errand." Then I made my way into the kitchen.

Joan was a few steps behind me. Feeling her hot on my trail, I turned around and said, "Do you want something?"

She walked up to me and got right in my face. With slanted beady eyes, she hissed, "While you're asleep tonight, I'm gonna come into your room and slit your throat."

I just looked at her pathetically, snickered, jingled the keys in her face, and then took flight. I didn't think much about it. I just passed it off as another heated episode in our day-to-day living. I was getting used to them. But later that evening, when I talked with Steve, he was gravely concerned.

"You know, sweetheart, she's not thinking clearly. The tension between the two of you is so escalated, she just might be crazy enough to do something like that."

I laughed. "No, she wouldn't do anything like that to me. She's my sister."

"Laura, she's not thinking clearly. And neither are you. She's projecting all her anguish onto you right now. She just might."

I hadn't been thinking in terms of Joan being in a psychological crisis. I was only focused on her physical crisis, the stroke, and the effects it had on her ability to think and rationalize. Steve reminded me again, that the recent trauma in her life was causing her to act irrationally. She was losing everything around her and saw me at the hand of the wheel. He went on to explain the common underlying triggers that compromise a person's mental health: trauma, stress, anxiety, and emotions.

"And continuous exposure to those triggers," he told me, "as in Joan's case, *can* push a person beyond their breaking point, causing them to react in ways they typically wouldn't." Steve recommended I leave the house that evening. "Just for the night," he suggested, "until things blow over."

He assured me she wouldn't harm her children, but convinced me I should take her threat a bit more seriously. I called Dad to see if I could stay with him for the night, but he wasn't home. So I called my mother.

I hadn't talked to Mom in a while. It was our pattern since my teenage years. We'd get into these huge arguments, say things we really didn't mean, and then not talk for a while. We were slow to forgive one another. The longest span of time we spent not talking was about a year. At some point one of us, usually me, would break the ice. She held grudges and could go for years not talking to someone. She hadn't talked with her only sister for almost fifteen years. All her family was like that. I couldn't even remember what our last argument was about.

Mom lived on the second floor of an apartment complex in the town of Bridgewater, not far from my sister. Since my previous visit last summer, Mom had sold the family home and moved into a two-bedroom apartment. The house was too big for her to manage on her own. "I'm simplifying my life," she told everyone.

When I arrived at her front door, I stood for a moment staring at the wreath of silk flowers and baby's breath. I reached out and touched the white felt dove perched on the vine, smiling as I remembered Mom coming home excited with her new purchase many years ago in my youth. It was the first time I knocked on the door of her new home.

After she gave me a quick tour, we sat at the dining room table sipping tea. I ran my fingers along the glossy white-lace tablecloth, etching the floral design, as I listened to her talk about her work as a banquet waitress at the country club. She surrounded herself with the things she loved: the cherry wood curio cabinet that displayed her mother's floral vintage teacups; a mahogany grandfather clock her dad had helped her buy; and framed pictures of her kids and grandchildren, which hung on the white walls.

She was a tall, beautiful, svelte woman with hazel eyes. She had attended modeling school in her late teens, learning the art of poise and beauty. She was up on the latest fashions and prided herself on her appearance. After I had explained the reason for my late night visit, she sipped the last of her tea, put her cigarette out in the lead crystal ashtray, and then stood up.

Biting her lower lip, while shaking her head vigorously from side to side, she said, "I don't want to get involved, Laura. *Please*, I don't want to get involved."

"I'm not asking you to get involved. I'm just trying to tell you something's wrong with your daughter. She's very sick right now. Don't you want to know your daughter's ill?"

"No, I don't want to get involved," she repeated. Then she reached for her tan leather purse hanging on the cane high-back dining room chair and said, "I need to go out for a few minutes. I'll be right back." And she was gone.

I looked at the ticking grandfather clock in the living room; it was almost 10:45 p.m. *Where's she going?* I walked over to the gold tapestry loveseat, sat down, picked up the *Good Housekeeping* magazine from the marble coffee table, and thumbed through it, waiting for her return.

Twenty minutes later, she reappeared in the doorway with a six-pack of Miller beer cradled under her arm. My heart sank with disappointment as I sat slouched on the loveseat watching her, as I had so many times before, pull a tall frosted beer glass from the freezer, pour the ale from the dark amber bottle into the tilted glass, light up a cigarette, and numb out.

Not long afterwards, I was lying in Mom's guest bed with tears leaking from my tightly closed eyes, feeling that old familiar pain of hurt and abandonment. Added to that was a deep longing to be bonded, to be held by the woman I hated the most. The thing was, I really needed my mom. I needed a shoulder to cry on. I needed her to put her loving arms around me and tell me everything was going to be all right. It made me woozy, the memories that lived on in my mind, of all the times I had needed her, of all the times she had numbed out, of all the times she hadn't been there for me.

We all find ourselves at one time or another in messy, complex situations. Why was I the one taking care of my sister and not her? I don't know why I thought maybe, just maybe this one time she'd be available, in a different way. But she wasn't. And I was left feeling the deep aching pain inside I had tried so many years to hide, my wanting her to unlock the door to my lonesome vacant heart.

# We Have A Plan

I finally found an outpatient rehabilitation facility in Braintree, only thirty minutes away. They had a "return to life" program, which specialized in rehabilitation for stroke patients that focused on cognitive retraining. It was a one-year, eight-hour-a-day program, Monday through Friday. They even had a service van that picked patients up and dropped them off every day.

Dad took Joan to the center, where they met with the program facilitator. It was expected she would start the program July first, the day after her thirtieth birthday.

She didn't want to go.

"We're trying to help you," Dad told her, when he arrived at her house late one morning to take her on the interview. "I know it probably doesn't look that way, but you need to trust me on this one, dear."

"But I want to stay here with my kids," she told him, with tears in her eyes.

"I know, dear. But you can't. You're sick. You need help. You need to do this for your children. It's only for a year," he said, smiling bravely, trying to convince her.

She listened to him. We all did. Dad wasn't much of a meddler. He stood back on the sidelines, observing the events of our lives. When we sought him for advice, he was rational and tried to offer different perspectives. Ultimately he supported our decisions, even if they were contrary to his opinion. But every once in a while, even when we didn't seek his counsel, if he had something of value to say, he wasn't afraid to speak it. And you were a fool if you didn't listen to him, because most often, he was right on the money.

Since Dr. Gordon advised us that Joan shouldn't live on her own, Dad came up with a plan.

"I have an extra bedroom, Laura's old room. You can stay with me for the next year until you complete the program," he told her, sitting with her at the kitchen table after they returned from their visit to the center.

They were statements, not questions. She didn't have a voice in the matter, and she knew it. It was a difficult moment for her. She looked as if she was about to cry. But she didn't. Instead, she squeezed her eyes tightly shut and then puckered her lips together. She didn't say much. She just went along with it all. But occasionally, when it was just she and I, she'd snarl at me and scream, "I hate what you're doing to me!"

I never responded. I couldn't. There was nothing I could say. She didn't have the ability to understand what was really going on, and I was just plain worn out from it all. Ever bit of my attention and focus went towards finding the answers, to get us through each and every step. While all along I was secretly hoping and praying for an end soon.

Since Joan couldn't live on her own, Dad didn't want the burden of managing and holding on to her house. He insisted on selling it. Joan loved the house and was understandably upset having to give it up. Since I had a real estate background, Dad asked me to help get it on the market, right away.

When Dad told her he was putting the house up for sale, she blamed me. "You're taking everything away from me!" she shouted.

*Didn't she see I was the one trying to fix it all?*

Dad called me one afternoon, shortly before the kids arrived home from school.

"Your Aunt Margie and Uncle John offered to take Lilly for the year."

"You sound pleased," I told him. For the first time since Joan's stroke he sounded untroubled.

"It's more relief than anything. Margie and John are a godsend to us right now in our time of need," he replied.

Uncle John was Dad's younger brother. He and his wife, Margie, were both in their late fifties. They owned a large split level home with a swimming pool in a quiet wooded development in a small town close to Dad. Aunt Margie had been a nurse for over thirty years and my sense was, she missed having little ones around. The maternal instincts came natural to her. Her temperament was patient, kind, and loving. Uncle John had retired early as a schoolteacher. He had a lucrative side hobby selling baseball cards and had been a gentle church-going man all his life. They were home all the time. And their five grown children, along with their respective partners, were always around as well.

Lilly had never met them. Dad took her over to their home the following afternoon. Lilly was an easy one. She, like her mom when she was little, loved people. She was sweet and easily amused. Most found her playful and adorable.

Piece by piece it was all coming together.

"I'm not sure what to do about Timmy and Tessy," I told Dad over the phone one evening, after everyone had gone to bed. "I called their dad's relatives, some of ours, and spoke with Timmy's best friend's mom to see if she knew anyone who might be interested in taking care of them. I even spoke with someone at the social service agency who suggested foster care."

"Foster homes for the kids?" Dad interrupted.

"Yeah, but I'm not sure it's a good idea. I don't know much about the foster care system. Some of the stories in the news are a bit scary. It feels like a huge gamble. What do you think?"

"God, Laura. I don't know."

There was a pause.

"Have *you* thought about taking care of them yourself?" he asked.

I jumped off the sofa, standing firmly to my feet. With my breath shallow and hard, I said, "What are you thinking? I can't do that! I just moved in with Steve. What am I supposed to do, take them to California? How would I care for them? I'm not a mother!"

I was upset he would even broach the subject. In truth, the idea had never, ever, entered my mind.

"It was just a thought, Laura. You don't need to get so upset," he said.

"Please, just drop it Dad," I insisted, before we hung up.

# Change of Heart

I couldn't let them go into a foster home, I just couldn't. I talked with Donna, a social service agency rep over the phone, just to get a better glimpse into the foster care system. After we exchanged details, the stories I had in my head about abusive foster parents changed. I felt more confident with the agency's protocols for screening and monitoring parents.

"The thing is," I said finally, "I don't want them separated. They *need* to stay together. Is that possible?"

"It's highly unlikely," she replied. "Most often we separate kids based on housing availability. It's rare to find a foster parent willing to take two kids in simultaneously."

After we hung up, I walked outside into the backyard, and sat on the white plastic lawn chair. I stared up at the gray clouds crossing the sky, as Ruby sat at my feet, gazing up at me with her big, brown, sad eyes. I felt agitated, even angry, to the point that I wanted to scream out at someone or something. Timmy and Tessy had never been away from each other. Not ever. It didn't seem fair, the injustice the two of them had already experienced in their short, little lives.

It was bad enough Joan had fallen for a man who was a loser in many respects. Wayne, Timmy and Tessy's dad, had had numerous run-ins with the law, had never been able to hold down a steady job, had had a long history of drug abuse, and add to that list, since he'd been a parent, he fully lived up to the reputation of a deadbeat dad. Joan had not one, but two children with that man who in no way, had ever been available to her or their children. She kept hoping and praying he'd change, but that never happened. It rarely does.

Knowing young boys tend to idealize their fathers, as Timmy did his, Joan had tried to overlook Wayne's deficiencies, focusing on the importance of her son maintaining contact with his father. Every year Joan invited Wayne to Timmy's birthday party. On Timmy's third birthday, he showed up. After a half hour, he pulled Timmy aside, crouched down in front of him and said, "I'll be right back, I'm just gonna run to the store to get a pack of smokes. I'll come right back."

But he never returned.

As the afternoon turned into dusk, Joan found Timmy standing on the sofa, his elbows resting on the windowsill, peering out onto the street, waiting for his dad to return. The next day, Joan found him again, sitting on the sofa, staring out, and waiting. And the next day after that, and the next one after that.

I know we all have flaws, and some of us are walking around this great big earth with troubles that are too burdensome for any one soul to handle. I try my best not to berate anyone. But I'd never been able to hold back when it came to that man. Because the next time Timmy saw his dad, a year later, on his fourth birthday, Wayne did the same thing to his son. Again, he told him he'd be back after he ran out to the store to buy cigarettes.

Overhearing the conversation and sensing the trauma it could cause Timmy, Joan excused herself from the party, followed Wayne out to his truck, and told him not to come by, ever again. It tore her up inside seeing her son go through that anguish. Not only were Timmy and Tessy without their dad, but soon, very soon, they'd be without their mom. It felt as if it would be an unnecessary hardship for them to be separated from one another.

So I decided to take them back to California for the year.

Dad was forever saying, "Check your motives." So I did. And the only true answers I could come up with were, first, it's my nature to be responsible and dependable. I tend to lean toward wanting to do the *right* thing. I couldn't picture myself back in my sunny California life with the possibility of the kids feeling abandoned, scared, and unhappy in foster homes.

But the more compelling reason for taking them was that the ghosts of my childhood had come knocking on my door. There was the time when I was six, maybe seven, somewhere around Tessy's age, when *my* mother went into the hospital. I came home from school one spring afternoon, and she was gone. My mommy ceased to exist for a time that felt like forever, leaving an empty hole in my heart.

My nana, my mom's mum, was a beautiful, robust, good-hearted woman who, in keeping with her Irish legacy, believed all of life's problems could be settled over a cup of tea. The day my mother went into the hospital, I saw Nana's big, blue Impala parked in front of our house from the school bus stop up the street. I ran all the way home so I would be the first one in her lap.

She was sitting at the kitchen table sipping a cup of Lipton tea. She sat my brothers and I down at the table, placed a plate of homemade chocolate chip cookies in front of us, and poured us each a tall glass of milk. With her long silky fingers, she pulled a blue lace handkerchief from under her dress sleeve. While rubbing it with both her hands, she looked up at us and said, "Your mum's in the hospital. She'll be okay. But you need to be brave and strong and help out by being good little children."

She nodded her head while cracking a faint smile. That's all I remember. She helped us each pack a suitcase and off we went to live with relatives until our mother was well again.

My older brother Brad and I stayed with our Aunt Elaine and Uncle Dick. It was okay because we knew them well, they were nice people, and they had kids around our age we liked to play with. They lived in a huge white colonial house on a lake where hundreds of red and yellow tulips lined the walkway down to the shore. Mostly I loved hanging out with my cousin Diane, who was a couple of years older than me. We sat for hours at the pink Formica kitchen table making love-bead necklaces together, and she taught me how to play Twister barefoot on her front yard. On Saturday mornings she took me to the park, where I learned to sing Jeremiah was a Bullfrog from soulful teenagers who played guitars and wore patched faded blue jeans. So in many ways my stay with my relatives while my mother was in the hospital was somewhat of an adventure for me. But in the secret chambers of my heart, pools of teardrops gathered, as my mommy seemed alive only in my memory.

I couldn't let Timmy and Tessy go into foster homes. Maybe my intention to take them was to compensate for my own childhood loss. It's possible, I suppose, that I was reacting to the whispering voices of the abandonment and anguish I had felt so long before. When I finally stopped telling myself all the reasons I couldn't take them, I was flooded with the memories of the little girl who still lived in me. She was scared and saddened by the memory of the distance and separation from her own mommy those many years ago. Though I had longed for different memories, I became present with the emptiness and heartache of the past that still lived in me. Eventually my resistance in taking the kids back to California with me vanished.

Steve and I talked it over, well, sort of.

"I've decided to take them back to California with me. I don't know what else to do. I can't let them go into foster homes. It just doesn't feel like the right thing to do," I told him over the phone one evening.

"It sounds like you've already come to a decision," he said.

There was a long silence.

"What's the matter? You don't have anything else to say?" I asked.

"You've already made up your mind. What's left for me to say?"

"What do you mean?" I asked.

"Don't you think you should've discussed this with me first? You're making choices about both our futures without consulting with me." He remained calm and rational, though I knew he was bothered.

"But, what am I supposed to do? I can't let them go into foster homes, I can't. You know I've been trying to find someone to take care of them, and I haven't been able to." I knew I was defending my reasons. He knew it too.

"You're making decisions that affect me, without talking with me."

"What am I supposed to do? Please, tell me what I should do?" I said, almost insistent.

"It's a tough one, Laura, I know. But I don't think you should take on the responsibility. They're not your children. They're not *your* responsibility."

"I *can't* let them go into foster homes. I just can't," I said wearily.

"I need to be with this on my own for a while. We can talk more about it later, but I need you to know that I don't like it," he said again, before a long deafening silence.

## Some Needed Help

I did something I never could have imagined I would ever do. Not able to fully comprehend what was happening in my, now *our* life, I saw a psychic (an intuitive). I was hoping to find clarity and understanding into the situation at hand. I figured it couldn't hurt.

I saw Lois in her attic home office. The room was soothing to my soul with sloping walls painted a pleasing translucent lilac and various wall hangings of angels in thick museum gold picture frames. Behind her desk was a child-size white marble statue of a goddess strumming a harp. A bouquet of fresh long-stemmed red roses stood in a thick glass vase in the center of a round glass coffee table, with a faint smell of rose misting the air.

Lois was an older, round, pleasant woman, with a heart-shaped face and an easy smile. She offered me a cup of chamomile tea before we began our session. She reminded me of an old friend; I immediately felt relaxed in her presence as I sat opposite her in an armchair covered with a fuzzy royal blue blanket.

She didn't ask any questions and began by saying, "You're in a time of powerful transformation."

*I figured that out all on my own, thank you very much.* Okay, I knew I was being a bit cynical, but I was hoping for some *real* answers, ones I could wrap my practical mind around. I listened intently as she talked about my own shortcomings and my childhood woundings that were resurfacing for healing. She explained that by being with Timmy and Tessy, I'd be delving into different parts of myself that had gone unexplored. She shed light onto the bigger reason that the situation was presenting itself, an opportunity to exercise and develop trust, or as she put it, "the trust muscle."

What stuck out for me was when she told me to just take care of the kids. That's it, that's all I needed to do.

"Listen," she said, with a soothing voice, as she leaned closer into me, "I understand you're scared. And I know this sounds a bit strange for you, but all you need to do is focus on the needs of the children. Every day. Just tend to their needs. By taking care of the children, God will provide and take care of the rest."

I jerked my head back, giving her a look that said, *you're kidding me, right? I paid all this money and you're telling me God is going to take care of us?* She reached for my hand, and turned her eyes up to the heavens. I'd like to say her warm, gentle touch transformed me into a believer, but that wasn't the case.

I was wrought with fear and uncertainty over our future. Any amount of confidence I had gathered in the years as a professional in the business world seemed now to be far out of reach. After being in the throes of my sister's crisis for over a month, I felt depleted and unsure of myself. Everything was happening much too fast; my life was running on autopilot. *I* was the one in crisis, and I didn't know how to be with myself any longer, let alone how to ease into the insurmountable changes I knew lay ahead.

I, we, were soon to be traveling back to California. I tried to imagine the unfolding of our lives, but every fumbling attempt drove me deeper into a state of worry, even panic. *Where are we going to live? How will I financially support us?* I had some money saved, but certainly not enough to support us all for the next year. I'd always been able to take care of myself, but now I had two children to support. I didn't know how I was going to manage it all. And the new life I was beginning with Steve, too seemed to be crumbling away like an old ruined building.

As the days unfolded, Steve was clear during our nightly telephone conversations that it was not an option for the children to live with us. And he didn't want to move out of the home he'd been happily living in for years.

"It's not part of our plan," he told me.

"But they're my family. I want *us* to be a family, the four of us," I said, sitting on the edge of my bed, my voice cracking from the vulnerability I was feeling.

"Laura, I need to set some boundaries. It's *your* decision to take them. *You* made that choice. I've already told you I'll support you as best I can. But this is not what I want for us, for myself. We've talked about this. I understand your focus and attention is now on your sister's kids. Please respect that *my* priority is on my work right now. I don't want to raise someone else's kids at this time in my life."

How could I argue with that? I understood his perspective, yet I wanted more from him. The kids and I hadn't even set foot on California ground, and he was already voicing the impending distraction he felt us to be. Earlier in our relationship we had talked about the possibility of having children. Someday, maybe, if it was what we both wanted. It wasn't a big yes for either of us. But certainly it wasn't now, not like this.

Since I was a young adult, having children seemed like a future possibility, when I wasn't tormented by my own maternal ambivalence. Even though Billy, my former husband, who had twelve siblings, was eager to have children and start a family, for me it had never seemed to be the right moment. I had plenty of time, right? I was part of a generation of young, professional women who waited until their later years to settle into family life. *I hadn't reached baby-making time in my life yet*, I told myself over and over again.

But the prospect of parenting Timmy and Tessy began shifting my views somewhat. I wanted to create something for them, or with them. After all, they were *my family*. I hoped Steve would have a change of heart, but he didn't see it my way. As a result, our relationship began to feel a bit sketchy as tension mounted on both sides.

In the late evening after my session with Lois, as the moon moved toward its fullness, I lay in bed, as the gentle breeze of summer rustled outside my window. My body was still while my mind raced. The lingering thought of God taking care of us refused to let my mind sleep.

The word "God" was rarely spoken in my family. My experience and knowledge of God came from the many years of parochial schools I attended. The expression and sometimes threats of God had oftentimes come out of the mouths of iron-fisted nuns. Their God, a longhaired white bearded man who descended from the vault of heaven, was a wrathful God. What left a not-so-positive lasting impression on me happened when I was in high school. Rumor had it that a classmate found herself pregnant. She was condemned to sit alone day after day in a dark, private room in the back of the library. The forced penance by our elders for a teenager's sins made me realize I could never hold true to their teachings. I felt somewhat jaded by it all. After I left high school, I didn't spend any time at all contemplating God.

Then Steve introduced me to Agape, an international spiritual center founded by Michael Bernard Beckwith. The organization, based on the New Thought-Ancient Wisdom tradition of spirituality, has as its vision, a movement based on love and peace. "Agape," which in Greek means *unconditional love*, is believed to be the essence of God. Since being with Steve, I had begun to wrestle with the idea of a spiritual life, my spiritual life. It was new territory for me. I had thought of church, meditation, yoga, and pilgrimages to India as the form and foundation of spiritual life. But I began to wonder, *Could it be something more?*

I knew I wanted to live more spiritually, but didn't understand what living a spiritual life meant to me. I'd spent years busying myself, listening to false voices scrambling around in my mind, pursuing things I thought would make me happy. Mostly I had distracted myself—from myself, I guess. I'd been bringing God more into my consciousness over the past year being with Steve, but hadn't fully understood God's mystery and presence. Does anyone? I think it was Michelangelo who said, "God is in the details." Through my studies at Agape, I was learning God is everywhere—in the trees, in a baby's coos, even in the pain and anguish of an unexpected death of a loved one. I was creating new beliefs and was beginning to see God as the presence of love and life itself. I was coming to terms with, or awakening to God as a guiding force in one's life, a star that draws one inward, deeper into one's own life, into one's own heart.

But all I could see was what was in front of me; I was back with my family trying to tend to our broken, shattered lives. I knew I needed to admit my heart had grown cold and was in need of mending. I wanted to have faith or trust in God, to believe we were all in this for some higher purpose. I guess that's what faith is about, knowing God is with us and will prevail. Nevertheless, I didn't believe or have faith that God would provide and take care of us because I was full of fear. It wasn't fear of God; rather, I was afraid of the unknown.

# Goodbye

Joan and I sat on the living room couch with the kids and explained, as best we could, the happenings within all our lives: selling the only home they knew, their mommy going to live with their grandfather, Lilly living with relatives they didn't know, and them moving to California with me. We tried to keep it simple. But how does one go about doing so when everything about a situation is so utterly complex? I told Timmy and Tessy their move to California was an adventure. I tried selling them on the many new fun experiences they would soon have: a plane ride, visiting Disneyland, going to Universal Studios, swimming pools, and bike rides along the beach.

"But, will we see you, Mommy?" asked Tessy, her eyes welling with tears.

Joan sucked in her lower lip and looked away. She took a deep breath and held it in for as long as she could. After she exhaled, we all looked at her, expecting her to say something, but she didn't. Then a look of fright came over Tessy. Her body began to tremble. She started to cry. She leaped into Joan's lap, clamping her arms tightly around her mommy's torso.

Witnessing Tessy's distress, I jumped in and said, "Princess, Mommy won't be coming to California. She'll stay here and live with Papa so she can get well again."

"But when, when will we see you Mommy?" she asked, with tears streaming down her cheeks.

Still, Joan said nothing.

"Our plan is for you and Timmy to live with me for one year. That's all. You'll see your mommy next summer," I said slowly, softly, sitting on the floor with my hands pressed together in prayer between my knees.

Tessy didn't say a word. She sat in Joan's lap, burrowing her face into her mommy's chest, shaking her head as she continued to cry.

Timmy spoke up. "No way! I'm not going to California! I'm not leaving my school. I like my school. I have friends there. And I'm definitely not leaving my best friend, Ryan," all the time unrelentingly shaking his head no. He looked like a he-man hero standing stiff in his body, his legs spread wide with his arms crossed in front of his chest.

"We *have* to do this Timmy. You don't have a choice. Your mommy is sick and needs time to get well."

He threw his arms down with his hands clenched into fists, shaking his head vigorously no, as he stomped his foot repeatedly on the floor while shouting, "No! It's not fair!"

"I know it's not fair. But you'll make new friends in your new school in September," I said, kneeling next to him on the floor.

"It's not fair!" he shouted again, flailing his arms.

"I know. But we *have* to do this."

"Where we gonna live? Where are we going to school?" he asked suspiciously, with his arms once again folded in front of his chest.

"I'm not sure yet. We'll figure it out. We'll figure it all out *together*. We're going to be a team, the three of us, just like all of you are a team with your mommy. It'll all work out Timmy, I promise. I told you I'd take care of you. You need to trust me." I placed my hand around his waist. He angrily shrugged his shoulders and pulled away.

"But who'll say our prayers and read bedtime stories?" Tessy asked, sniffling. She looked up at Joan. Her face was covered with tears.

"I will, Princess. I'll read bedtime stories to the both of you, every night. And we'll say prayers together and pray for you and Timmy and Lilly to be back home with your mommy." I reached my hand toward her. She refused my touch and cuddled in closer to her mom like a newborn kitten squirming to suckle its mother's milk.

"Mommy, what about Ruby? Who'll take care of Ruby?" asked Timmy, with a concerned face. "Ruby's part of our family too. You didn't mention her. Who'll take care of her?"

Ruby was indeed a valued family member. She was the loyal and lovable cocker spaniel who'd been in the family for almost as long as Tessy. With all I was managing, I'd forgotten about Ruby. I suppose I could've made up some kind of story, right there on the spot, like she was going to live with a neighbor or friend. But lying in moments such as these had never been my strong point. Because I wanted the kids never to distrust what I said, I always, always told them the truth. And I tried to keep it as simple as possible.

So I ended up telling them, "I forgot about Ruby." I assured them we would find a loving home for her, too.

Over the next few days it was a project the three of us worked on together. They came up with different ideas and solutions on finding a "foster home" for Ruby, but with people they knew. Since school was coming to an end, they each made announcements to their classmates on the last day of school, like a show and tell. They glued pictures of Ruby onto colored construction paper and wrote in black marker an explanation under each picture describing what she was doing in the photo.

They also wrote a list of all her good qualities, which they read out loud in school: She eats everything in her bowl, she always scratches at the door letting you know she needs to go outside to go to the bathroom, and she likes watching TV. We also talked with neighbors who knew Ruby.

In the end, Ruby went to live with Timmy's best friend, Ryan and his family. The day Ryan and his mom came to pick up Ruby and all her accessories, Timmy and Tessy stood in the driveway, waving goodbye until the van was out of sight. Then they turned to one another, shook hands, gave each other a high-five, and a satisfied nod.

Lilly had already been settling into her new life. Dad spent the last week taking her over to Uncle John's house every day, gradually transitioning her. She loved being there. She received lots of attention and gifts of new clothes, stuffed animals, and toys. The heat of the summer was upon us, and she often came home with exciting stories of swimming pool fun.

A few days before we left, Dad, Joan and I went to court, where in the dark, vacant courtroom, Joan signed power of attorney for all her three children over to Dad. By that time the strain of the crisis had injured us all. What little conversation we had on the drive to the courthouse, turned into dead silence on the ride home. Joan sat in the front seat staring out the passenger side window looking hopeless and gloomy. I saw her pain, but couldn't be there for her. I was angry, even livid. All the fights and words we had spoken to one another had taken their toll on me—and her as well. Toward the end, we had little to say to one another.

I wasn't speaking to my mother either. Again. It was *my* choice this time, not hers. "I don't want to get involved" recordings replayed over and over in my head. I was pissed she wasn't available to help during *our* family's crisis. Her avoidance methods had always pained me, but I was deeply disappointed when she stood on the sidelines this time without lending a finger. I wanted her to do something, anything. My only coping mechanism was to keep my distance, both in words and in physical contact.

Dad, on the other hand, was extremely appreciative of all the things I'd done and thrilled I was taking the kids back to California with me.

"I know I could never repay you for all you've done. But if there's something I can do for you, a small gift, a token of my appreciation…" he offered.

Steve suggested the kids and I needed time to heal and bond after all the stress we'd been through. One of his closest friends, Lori, who lived in Northern California, was at her summer home in Maui, with her son, Christopher, who was Timmy's age. Though Lori had never met Timmy and Tessy, she graciously invited us to join them, offering the children companionship.

"It'll be good for you, the kids, and us to have some fun together. It'll also give us time to figure things out," Steve suggested.

Dad was a bit surprised with my request to go to Maui, though more than willing to financially provide for it.

On the last day of June, our entire family gathered for a luncheon at a local restaurant to celebrate Joan's thirtieth birthday. It was also the day Timmy, Tessy and I left for California. I wish I could say there was a crowd of joyful people at our luncheon. Even though all the kids received great send-off gifts, the undertone was fairly subdued. They all clung to their mother, counting the hours, then minutes remaining with her.

I made the stupid mistake of suggesting Tessy wear my favorite childhood dress. It had been among the items Mom gave me when I toured her new apartment. She had presented me with a box containing things she had gathered when clearing out the basement of our family home. We sat at her dining room table as I opened the box, an immediate gateway into my childhood. Among the many items was a white ceramic angel holding a candle, a gift I had given Mom for Christmas when I was in first grade. I also found a cracked white plaster print of my hand with a few remaining speckles of green glitter, which I had made in kindergarten, as well as my bronze baby shoes. And there was a picture of me sitting in my Nana's lap on my first birthday, wearing a yellow ruffled dress and matching bonnet.

Mom carefully wrapped my puffy pink chiffon dress, which I had worn for my fourth birthday party, in white tissue paper and tied it with a pink ribbon. I remember feeling like a fairy princess when I wore that dress. It had a pink embroidered eyelet hem and a four-inch pink satin ribbon that tied in a huge bow in the back. Mom told me she had saved the dress for me to give to my own daughter someday. I thought I'd spiff it up a bit for Tessy by adding lace flowers to the neckline and waistband. I bought Tessy a short white cotton slip with a ruffled bottom, fancy pink lace eyelet socks, and new black patent leather shoes for Joan's birthday celebration. I did it partially because Lilly had been coming home from her visits at Uncle John's with beautiful new clothes, and I knew Tessy was a little jealous. I also did it because I wanted Tessy to be my little girl, the daughter I never had.

Even though Tessy and I planned a week ahead for her to wear the dress, on the day of the event, she announced, "No, I don't wanna wear it. I wanna wear my blue skirt, the one Mommy gave me for Christmas."

I was crushed, heartbroken when she told me she didn't want to wear it. I finally bribed her into wearing it and felt pleased, but for only a very short time. After we sang happy birthday to Joan at the restaurant, Tessy had a breakdown. She tried sitting on her mother's lap, but Lilly was there and didn't want to share her real estate with anyone. Lilly yelled and screamed, "Get away!" as she shook her head, all the while pushing and kicking Tessy away with her chubby legs, whenever Tessy tried to snuggle close to her mom.

In a state of reaction, Tessy kicked off her shoes and then pulled off her socks, throwing them across the room. With a scowl eye, she tugged and tore at the neckline because it was too tight or too itchy or too something. Next, while clenching her teeth, she yanked all the long pink satin ribbons out of her hair. All along she'd muttered under her breath, between clenched teeth, "This looks *stupid*! I hate it! I hate myself!" It wasn't long before the dress lay abandoned on the floor of the restaurant.

As much as I tried to console her, reason with her, or try to control her behavior, there was absolutely nothing I could say or do to help the situation. Half an hour later, after she had had private time with her mommy, she was prancing around in her white slip, modeling the new blue-flowered quilted backpack her mother had just given her.

It took forever for us to say our goodbyes, or at least it felt that way to me. While standing at the boarding gate at the airport, I tried ushering the kids along, like a mother duck herding her ducklings. But every two steps they took toward the plane, they'd turn around and run straight back into their mother's arms.

For me, boarding that plane offered a simple doorway to peace. I did my best, but I couldn't pretend I wasn't happy to finally have the distance I longed for, from my sister, my mother, and my family in general. Things felt a little less complicated with only the two kids. It was obvious to everyone that going back home to California was a welcome change for me.

# I Miss My Mommy

Steve met us at the LAX airport, and together we all flew to Hawaii. The kids were excited, fidgeting with the knobs, opening and closing the airplane window shade, getting in and out of their seats to walk down the isle. I packed plenty of travel-size games like Connect Four, Trouble, and Checkers, to keep them entertained and quiet. But by the time we hit the ground, eight hours later, they wanted—and needed—to move. While walking through the Maui airport terminal, we made it as far as the atrium when Timmy suddenly stopped short and stared at the giant palm tree in front of him.

"Wow, cool!" he said, as his eyes grew big and bright.

It was the first time he'd ever seen a palm tree. He ran ahead of us, jumped over the tile bench and approached the tree by trying to mount it, wrapping both arms and legs around it. As Steve, Tessy and I walked closer to the tree, Steve came to an abrupt halt, placed his black canvas carry-on bag on the tile floor, shook his head disapprovingly, and said loudly, "Get off the tree, Timmy," as he waved his arms motioning Timmy to return to us.

With Tessy's hand in mine and while still maintaining my pace, I told Steve, "He's okay. Just let it go."

Timmy eventually caught up to us. While tugging at my sleeve, Timmy said, "Auntie, did you see me? I was a monkey climbing a monkey tree."

"Yeah, Timmy, I saw you. Looks like you were having fun. Why don't you stay with us now," I told him.

Timmy ran up to Steve, almost tripping and asked, "Did you see me, Uncle Steve? Did you see me climbing the monkey tree?"

Steve stopped again, turned to Timmy and said, "I dub you Monkey Boy," as he stretched out his right arm, pretending to hold a sword, anointing Timmy on both shoulders. "That's what we'll call you, Monkey Boy." Then he chuckled before resuming his pace. Timmy beamed a smile from ear to ear.

Since we had flown with children, we were the first to board and exit the plane and the first to arrive at the baggage claim area. There was only a scattering of people about. As we approached the empty baggage carousel, I stopped to look through my bags, in search of my sunglasses. While I wasn't looking, the kids ran ahead and hopped onto the carousel, thinking it was some kind of an amusement ride, because they'd never seen one before. They were joyfully shouting and laughing as they tried standing on the moving steel conveyor belt. I didn't have much of a problem with them playing on it, especially since no one was around. In fact, I thought it was funny watching them trying to maintain their balance. I was glad to laugh at something, to find amusement in life again. Steve on the other hand, felt they were being unruly.

"Boundaries, Laura. They need to learn boundaries," he insisted, shaking his head with raised eyebrows. "And you're the one who has to teach them."

But I didn't see it that way. I once read a story of a man who was traveling by train with his two young children. The kids were bickering and elbowing one another to the point it was bothersome to the other passengers. When one of those passengers finally spoke up and said something to the father, the dad responded by saying, "Oh, I'm sorry. I didn't even notice. We just came from the hospital where their mother died a few hours ago."

Reading that story made me realize we really don't know the stories other people carry in their hearts. What we present to the world through our actions is often the surface stuff we're all trying to muddle through. But when we dig down a little deeper, with each person, there's usually a heart-wrenching life experience they carry that can oftentimes profoundly blow our minds and open our compassionate heart.

I felt in some way I was that parent whose children had just lost the single most important person in their lives. I knew their mother wasn't dead, but I didn't have a clue what was going on in their little minds. It didn't matter much to me when they jumped on the carousel or mounted a tree. I wanted to cut them some slack.

We arrived at Lori's home in the late afternoon. There at the edge of her property, where the earth met the sea, all the colors blazed in the sky. I inhaled a giant breath of fresh sea air, as my body remembered and relaxed. I smiled, feeling home again. I was returning to a place where Steve and I, not too long before, had had magical moments of lovemaking and long walks along the shore filled with laughter and plans for our future. I felt so grateful to be in the arms of the *Great Mother* again.

The children and I headed straight for the guest cottage, a simple two-bedroom bamboo house with sienna tile floors, pale yellow stucco walls, and natural dark wood ceiling beams. A yellow rustic metal ceiling fan hung in the center of the main room over a round wood dining table. The open sliding glass doors led to a gray-blue slate patio. For a moment, I was lost in the sound of seashell wind chimes tinkling in the soft waft of the tropical summer air.

"Hey, Tessy, look at the lizards on the wall," Timmy said, with excited eyes. He dropped his suitcase in the center of the room, cupping his hands as he crept closer to the wall.

"They're called geckos, and you'll see plenty of them on the island," I said, as I placed my purse and sunglasses on the dining table. Steve was in the main house, visiting with Lori and her houseguests, while I introduced the kids to our new home for the next month.

"Cool," said Timmy, as he and Tessy tagged along after me checking out the cottage.

"I like this place, Auntie," exclaimed Tessy, rolling her purple Pocahontas luggage into their bedroom.

"Can we go explore?" asked Timmy.

"Let's unpack first. Then once we've settled in, we can have a look around. Okay?" I didn't want us to be living out of suitcases. I felt it was important for them to feel safe and at home everywhere we went.

"You take that bed Tessy, and I'll take this one," said Timmy, as he pointed to each twin bed on opposite sides of the room. Tessy shook her head in agreement. "And since I'm taller, I'll take the top three drawers, and you take the bottom three. All right?" asked Timmy.

They quickly moved about the room, placing their clothes in the drawers, their shoes in the closet, and their pillows and stuffed animals on top of their beds. They hadn't been able to bring much with them. "Only two suitcases each, so choose wisely," I had told them while packing up their house. Timmy's greatest treasures were his collection of *Goosebumps* books, his new baseball glove that Steve and I had sent him for his eighth birthday that February, his 'must have' baseball cards, and his Game Boy. For Tessy it was her Barbies and accessories, her coloring and sticker books, and the jewel-framed picture of her with her mommy on her sixth birthday last summer.

After we had completed our unpacking, we walked out onto the grounds, where things grew lush and green. A rolling plush landscape of tall green grasses, palm and banana trees, exotic bird of paradise, and fragrant plumeria trees filled the terrain. The kids weren't all that interested in the lavish scenery, the ocean waters, the oversized hot tub, or the sound of a cascading waterfall in the distance. All they cared about was the sixty-foot solar heated salt-water swimming pool awaiting them.

It amazed me to witness their awe and wonderment over things I had long taken for granted. Their eyes lit up when they first saw the pool and the half-dozen kids already playing in it. Timmy couldn't contain himself; he wiggled and bounced uncontrollably, shaking his arms and hands feverishly, in anticipation of jumping in on a game of water volleyball Lori's son, Christopher, and his friends were playing. Tessy ran over to a huge green round plastic trash barrel containing flippers, snorkels, and neon-colored noodles. She dug down deep into the container with the eagerness of treasures awaiting her, like a child on Christmas morning.

"Auntie, I found two mermaid floaties," she yelled, waving the inflated plastic pink armbands in the air.

For the next two hours they played merrily in the pool, while I sat on a floral cushioned lounge chair, reading a book for the first time in almost six weeks.

After dinner, Steve suggested some "male time" for Timmy, so the two of them drove into town to run a few errands. Timmy had grumbled a couple of times to Steve how unfair it was for him to be constantly surrounded by *girls* while growing up in his family. Timmy and Steve shared an enthusiasm for baseball and whenever they were together, Timmy constantly asked Steve questions about the different games he'd attended and stadiums he'd visited over the years. Last summer, when

Steve joined me on my visit back East, Timmy had invited him to one of his little league games. When the dad who usually umpired didn't show up, Steve took his place. At home after the game, Steve and Timmy sat side by side at the dinner table, laughing and sharing stories about Steve's umpiring. It was clear that Steve enjoyed playing the "uncle" role.

Tessy seemed okay when she wasn't invited to go with Steve and Timmy to the store. I sat at the round dining table writing a grocery list for the shopping we planned to do the following morning. Tessy sat on the floor a few feet away, playing with her Barbies.

After some time had passed, Tessy crawled up to me. With her head slightly tilted and the tip of her right index finger resting on her lower lip, she uttered, "Auntie, I miss my mommy."

I looked down at her and noticed her eyes were watery, as her lips began to quiver. I put down my pen and picked her up in my arms, resting her head on my shoulder. While rocking her, I walked over to the yellow floral wicker sofa and sat her gently on my lap. I cradled her like a baby, with her face snuggled against my breast. With my left arm holding her body and my right hand supporting her head, I began rocking her side to side while she wept.

I took long, deep breaths, shushing her, "Shhh, everything will be all right, Princess. I'm right here. Shhh."

As I sat rocking her, memories of me at her age flooded my mind. My breathing became slow and long as my chest started to slightly shudder. Like Tessy, I too was feeling the fear and aloneness of when I was without my mommy many years ago, when she was sick, and I couldn't be with her. The memories were so strong and still alive in me, that for a moment, I actually felt them to be real. I felt myself to be both who I was in present time and the lonely little girl I had once been. As I sat there rocking Tessy, comforting her in her sadness, I too began to cry. And for a moment, I didn't feel separate as we clung to one another. I found myself crouched over, whispering melodically into Tessy's ear, or maybe it was to myself, "I miss my mommy. I miss my mommy," as we rocked and cried together for a very long time.

# Alone Time

While lounging at the pool the following day, I watched Timmy, who was swimming in the deep end of the pool with Christopher and a couple of his friends, taunt Tessy. He took a deep breath, pinched his nose shut with two fingers, swam under water over to the shallow end of the pool, positioned himself under the float Tessy was lying on, and flipped her upside down.

When I questioned him about it, he whined, "She's been bugging me and following me around. I need my alone time. I need time without *her* around."

Boy, could I relate. So I let him go back to the house, alone, to watch a televised baseball game. Two hours later he reemerged, happy and joyful again. That experience helped me to see how important it was for them to have some time apart.

I found a day camp for the kids to attend, Monday through Friday. It was a co-ed program with about twenty kids around the same age as them. They played sports and outdoor games like croquet, badminton, and horseshoes. They took local trips to the railroad station, pineapple plantation, and beach. They also had a ping-pong table and arts and craft time. I thought they'd be thrilled to go.

"It's not fair! Christopher gets to stay home. Why can't we?" Timmy protested every morning on the drive to the camp.

Christopher, Lori's only child, who was eight years old like Timmy, *did* get to stay home and play in the pool everyday with his friends. I knew Timmy and Tessy were making new friends with Christopher and his friends and that they wanted to be part of that playtime. I didn't blame them for not wanting to go to camp, but I *needed* time alone, away from them. Steve was only in Maui for ten days, and he and I needed to spend some alone time together. Day camp was the only way for me to create the space I desperately wanted. I hoped after the first few days they'd like it, or at least get used to it. But their complaining continued.

While they were at camp, Steve and I spent our time enjoying leisurely breakfasts, going for long walks along the beach, making love, and arguing. We argued about everything. We argued about the kids. We argued over our plans for the kids. And we argued about the lack of love making because of the kids.

During a stroll along the beach late one morning, Steve said, "You've changed. Where's the beautiful, fun woman I fell in love with? You're like an angry, stressed-out mother, with all your attention on the kids."

I thought once we were away from my family and in Hawaii, everything would be fine. I thought I'd have some time to myself. I thought the kids would settle down and not fight with each other. I thought, or hoped, Steve and I would be able to rekindle the love and affection we had shared only months earlier. Boy, did I have it all wrong. Not only were the kids still arguing with one another, but they also started hitting each other.

Like one evening, while I was in the kitchen cutting

tomatoes for a salad for dinner, I heard Tessy scream, "Auntie! Help!" I dropped the knife and ran into their bedroom. Tessy was lying on the floor with Timmy sitting on top of her. He was leaning over her with his knees pinning her shoulders, with his hands tightly gripping her wrists above her head. I didn't have a clue how to deal with that type of behavior.

And when Tessy wasn't in the pool, she demanded my full attention. She either wanted me to play with her or cuddle and rock her, all the time. She sobbed day after day because she missed her mommy so very much. I tried to give her as much love and attention as I could, but it was never ending.

One afternoon while I was holding and rocking Tessy's wet body by the pool, Timmy got out of the water, walked over to me and said, "You love *her* more than you love me."

It wasn't unusual for me to be holding and rocking the two of them for long periods of time. They continually needed and pulled on me in ways I'd never experienced before. So how could I be there for Steve? For us? I couldn't even be there for myself. I felt ratty looking, with my hair pulled back in a ponytail, wearing the same khaki shorts and black halter bra day after day. I didn't put any time and attention into my appearance. My daily hiking routine had stopped completely. I was constantly on edge with a daily "to do" list of the kids' needs: feeding them, bathing them, doing laundry, playing games, handling injuries, counseling their arguments. I felt utterly exhausted by the end of each day. I was far from feeling aroused and wanting hot, juicy sex.

And to make matters worse, on Thursday, Timmy and Tessy's fourth day at camp, Steve and I had a huge fight. Because of our arguing, we were half an hour late picking them up from camp. When we finally arrived on the scene, they were waiting outside in the wide grassy field by the picnic table. All the other children were gone. They were standing alone with the camp counselor. I jumped out of the car before Steve had a chance to put it in park. I started running, making my way toward them.

Timmy stepped up onto the picnic bench with his hands knotted in front of his chest and screamed, "You're late! Our mom was *never* late picking us up! *Never*!"

I dropped to my knees, gushing with apologies. But they had red in their eyes.

Tessy, who was standing on the grass under Timmy, squinted her eyes, placed both her hands on her hips, and shouted, "Yeah, you left us here! You forgot about us! I *hate* you! I *hate* both of you! You're *stupid*! You're both *stupid*!" She stomped both her feet repeatedly in a fit of rage, pointing and waving her index finger out toward us.

My heart was racing. With my mouth open, I looked over at Steve, shaking my head at him, looking for a hint what to do. He too was on his knees, a foot or so behind me.

He spoke up, "It's not your Auntie's fault. It's my fault. You can blame me for being late. You can get angry with me, but not your Auntie. It wasn't her fault."

"I don't care! I *hate* you both! It's *both* your fault!" Timmy yelled back, shaking his balled fists in the air while jumping on the bench.

For a moment, no one said a word.

"I have an idea you might like, Timmy," said Steve. "If it'll make you feel any better, you can take a swing at me."

I quickly glanced over at Steve, shaking my head left and right. He gave me a brief nod and wink, letting me know he knew what he was doing.

"I *hate* you!" Timmy screamed again, his face was red as he pointed at Steve.

"It's okay, Timmy. Really. You can hate me and be angry with me. It's okay. And if it'll make you feel any better, you can take a swing at me. I'm not kidding."

Even though Timmy was somewhat skeptical, he jumped down off the bench. Steve repositioned himself on the grass, kneeling in a way that made him eye level with Timmy. With both hands still clenched into fists, Timmy cautiously walked closer toward Steve.

Steve was slowly shaking his head yes, while saying, "It's okay, Timmy. It's okay."

When Timmy was about arm's length away, he stood face to face with Steve and while staring him square in the eyes, he took a deep breath in. Then he pulled his left arm back, took another deep breath, gritted his teeth, and with all his might, swung his arm forward and let Steve have it. He punched him smack in the left eye. As it turned out, he ended up giving him quite a shiner. Timmy stood motionless, staring at Steve. I wouldn't say Timmy was happy or even pleased with himself, but his rage was gone. He quieted down and his posture was softer, more relaxed.

Steve rubbed his eye and said, "Wow, that was quite a punch. Are you feeling any better?"

Timmy didn't say anything.

Steve then turned to Tessy, an eager spectator who had crept closer and was now about a foot or so away from me, and offered her the same opportunity. She took a few steps back, shaking her head no. But Timmy urged her on.

"Come on, Tessy. You can do it. It'll make you feel better. Just hit him. It's easy. Just do what I did," he advised, as he took a few steps in her direction, waving his hand for her to stand next to him.

Tessy warily, slowly, walked toward Timmy. Timmy took her by the hand and walked her closer to Steve. He stood behind her and while holding her shoulders, positioned her to where he had previously stood. He rolled her right hand into a fist, angled her body, lifted her chin, and took hold of her right elbow showing her how to take it back before thrusting it forward.

"Just like this," he said, moving her fist forward.

"You got it?" he asked.

"Got it," she replied, nodding her head.

When she was ready, she took a deep breath in and held it tight. Then she pulled her right arm back while biting her lower lip. She thrust her arm forward, but instead of hitting Steve, she threw both her arms around his neck, jumped into his arms, and sobbed heavily on his shoulder.

Steve hugged her tightly, rocking her gently, as he placed his chin on top of her head, saying, "It's okay, Tessy. I love you. It's okay." He too began to cry.

Moments later, we were all in the camp field crying and hugging and rolling around in the grass with one another.

Later that night, while curled up against Steve's sleeping body, my stomach churned as I thought how abandoned the kids must have felt at the day camp. My grief soon gave way to a feeling of having failed dismally in caring and protecting them, not only from life's pains and heartaches, but from me as well. I blamed myself.

Soft tears rolled down my checks. Silently, like a prayer, I whispered over and over again, *I'm so sorry. Please God, guide me to do what's right. Guide me to love and care for my little ones.*

The next morning, I walked into the kids' room to wake them up and get them ready for camp.

Still lying in bed, sleepy eyed, Timmy said, "Auntie, we don't wanna go back to camp. We don't like it there. Can you please not send us away? We'll be good, I promise."

Still standing in the doorway, I began to cry. I looked over at Tessy; she too was lying half awake in her bed, yawning. I managed to smile and waved my hand, motioning her to join us, as I walked over to Timmy's bed. I held the sheet up as she crawled in under it and snuggle up next to him. I knelt down and wiped the tears from my eyes as I silently kissed them on their cheeks, hugging them tightly together.

I sniffled and with a sigh, I said, "Okay. You don't have to go to camp any more. But I need some alone time. You know, like when you need time to yourself. And I need your help. Okay?"

They looked at each other and then back at me, and shook their smiling happy faces in agreement.

# Bamboo Forest

The day before Steve flew back to Los Angeles, Lori invited us to join her and a group of friends at the local waterfalls. She was generous that way, welcoming us into her home and daily activities. She was an experienced mother who was marvelously understanding and able to relieve my concerns effortlessly when needed. Like one morning, after cuddling with Tessy in bed, I discovered Tessy had head lice. Panicking, I ran to Lori, asking her what I should do.

Calmly, Lori replied, "Oh, that's common for kids. She probably got it at the day camp. It's easy to get rid of, so don't worry," before giving me specific instructions on how to deal with it properly. Lori was also helpful with parenting tips and how-to suggestions. The best piece of advice I learned from her on how to keep kids happy, "Is for them to be with other kids." So I always made a point to accept play dates when they came our way.

On our way down to the waterfalls, we took the most exhilarating hike through the thick majestic bamboo forest. I felt as if I were in heaven, scanning the forest floor, meandering beneath a dense canopy of plush fertile emerald woodlands. The trees were forty feet high, shooting straight up above into the clear crystal blue sky, with long, thin wispy jade-colored leaves hitting and fanning our brows. The huge hollow bamboo trees were natural wind chimes, clanking and clattering as we made our way along the thirty-minute hike in. It was a first for the kids. Everything was. They had never traveled outside Massachusetts. Here on the island with graceful green sea turtles, flying dolphins, and cascading rainbows, they were charmed beyond belief.

During our bamboo forest walk, Tessy, while leaping from rock to rock, elatedly called out, "It's like being in a *real* life fairy tale, Auntie. I feel like I'm a *real* princess walking through the magic forest."

We wound up being a group of fifteen, spread out along the massive black volcanic rocks with our blankets, towels, lunch packs, swimming gear, and suntan lotion. The waterfalls were along the road to Hana, the rainy side of the island, so we got caught in a twenty-minute downpour. We spent the entire rainstorm splashing and frolicking in nature's blue pool at the foot of the falls. At one point, as we were having swimming races in the rain, with the kids on our backs, Tessy shouted gleefully, "It's raining happy God tears!"

Eventually the sun peaked through the clouds and once again we were bathed in brilliant sunlight. We watched the miraculous creation of miniature rainbows as the sunbeams smiled into each raindrop perched on the gigantic tropical leaves. It made me think of the lines from William Blake's poem *Auguries of Innocence*: "To see a world in a grain of sand, / And a heaven in a wild flower, / Hold infinity in the palm of your hand, / And eternity in an hour."

The children were blissed out. We were all full of our best stuff; every one of us was steeped in luminous joy. For a moment I truly understood first hand what it meant to dance in the garden of wondrous delight with another. Not wanting the day to end, we decided to stay an extra half hour after everyone else left. As we made our way back to the car through the labyrinth, weaving and zigzagging over streams and rocks, with sharp bends and narrow curves, Steve, who was in the lead, suddenly stopped, turned around, and said, "I think we're lost."

"It's this way, Uncle Steve," said Timmy confidently, pointing to a clearing through the trees.

"Ummm, I'm not sure about that, Timmy. Let's you and I go up ahead and have a better look," he suggested.

He turned back to me and said, "Sweetheart, you and Tessy hang out here for a few minutes while we scout things out."

I'd been holding Tessy's hand most of the way. The moment Steve announced we were lost, she squeezed my hand hard and tight and then stood frozen while perched on a rock.

With a shallow breath, almost like she was gasping for air, she said, "I don't like to be lost, Auntie. I'm scared."

I bent over, reached my arms out toward her and said, "Come here."

She whimpered as she climbed up into my arms, gripping onto her blue quilted backpack, the one her mother had given her the day she left for California. She swung her bare legs around my waist, tightly clasping them at her ankles.

"It's okay, Princess," I said, kissing her forehead. "We'll find our way out of here very soon."

"But, I'm really scared, Auntie. I miss my mommy. I'm never gonna see my mommy again," she whimpered. Her face became flushed. She tucked her arms in under her chest, leaning against my breast as she laid her head on my shoulder.

I folded my brown hooded sweatshirt around her thin body, stretching it out before I zippered it up over her back, creating a womb for her to snuggle into.

"Oh, Princess, sure you will. You'll see your mommy again, I promise. Uncle Steve's going to get us out of here very soon."

I kissed the top of her head and rubbed her back in slow, rhythmic circles. Dusk was approaching. I sensed danger, knowing we only had, at best, twenty minutes before darkness was upon us. We hadn't brought flashlights and weren't prepared for nightfall. Silently, I too was a bit unnerved by it all.

The fear Tessy was displaying was not unknown to me. I was haunted by a memory of the time when I was around seven, when our family attended a party at my Aunt Elaine's home. Dad was a heavy drinker back then. When we finally left the party sometime around 1 a.m., Dad was pretty intoxicated. He drove a Chevy convertible, but he was too drunk to put the top up, so we drove the twelve-mile ride home with the top down. Mom sat in the front seat with our baby brother, Joey, on her lap. The four of us kids were huddled in the back seat. I was cold; my body shivered as my teeth chattered uncontrollably. I tucked my legs tightly up under my red sweeter and wrapped a towel around my feet to keep warm. Dad was swerving all over the road. Mom screeched, "Wake up, Bill!" a few times, as he almost fell asleep at the wheel. Crouched in the back seat of the car, my siblings and I didn't say a word, but held onto one another tighter than I'd ever known in my short life. Mom told us to go to sleep, "We'll be home soon," she said, trying to comfort and assure us. But I didn't feel comforted by her words. I was really scared.

I remember looking up at the stars zinging across the night sky. For a moment, the brilliant gleaming speckles high above us took my mind off the impending tragedy I feared. The natural world has a way of doing that. The mystery of the sparkling jewels in the pitch-black sky softened me somehow and gave rise to a softer, calmer voice within. Something changed as I gazed up into the luminous sky. My fears and doubts transformed into hope, and I began instead to pray we'd all make it home safely.

I didn't have an inkling how to find our way out of the bamboo forest. Tessy kept saying, "I'm scared, Auntie," over and over again. I tried to think of a way to calm her fear. I looked up into the sky, searching for a star, a guiding light, or a hopeful sign, just as I had done when I was a little girl. Just then, I remembered a song I learned during weekly service at Agape. I started to sing it out loud.

*I'm thankful, so grateful, I'm one with the spirit all around me. I'm thankful, so grateful, I trust in God.*

I sang it over and over again while rocking Tessy, hoping it would soothe and calm her down. Eventually, she stopped crying and with a little coaxing from me, she began singing that song with me. After a few moments, we were singing in harmony and the tension in her body softened and disappeared.

Just then, Michael, Lori's brother-in-law, who'd been at the waterfalls with us earlier, hollered out, "Steve! Laura! Timmy! Tessy!" from the road up above.

Hearing Michael's call, Tessy lifted her head up and with a sense of urgency, she squirmed her arm through the opening of the hooded sweatshirt, thrusting it up into the air, waving it fiercely, as she hollered back, "We're here, Michael! We're here!"

Then she turned her sun-kissed face toward me and said, "We've been saved, Auntie! We've been saved!" And grinning widely, she pulled her other arm out of the zippered sweatshirt and gave me a great big heartfelt hug around my neck.

# Forgiveness

It was Tessy's seventh birthday. Since Lori and her friends were expected to arrive at ten o'clock for a surprise birthday breakfast, I was up earlier than normal preparing for Tessy's special day. First, I blew up twenty-five royal blue balloons, her favorite color; tied long curly pink and purple ribbons on them; and then scattered them around on the floor of the guest cottage. Next, I decorated the dining room with pink, purple, and royal blue crepe paper, ribbons, and streamers. Then I made a "Happy 7th Birthday Tessy" sign on heavy pink construction paper with royal-blue glitter and hung it on her birthday chair, along with matching streamers and balloons. I made Tessy's favorite meal—pancakes—and added a handful of chocolate chips, topping it off with whipped cream and a blue candle in the shape of a 7. I bought her a sparkling rhinestone tiara that I set on top of the five wrapped gifts I carefully stacked on her birthday chair. Finally, on the edge of her plate, I placed a fragrant white orchid lei.

Then I stood back, looking at it all and wondered, *Is it enough? Will this make her happy? Or will she be sad because her mommy's not with her on her special day?* I was doing the best I could, but some days, it just didn't seem like it was enough.

Shortly after I completed my preparations, the telephone rang.

"Hey, Laura. Is Tessy there?"

"Hi, Joan. She's still asleep," I answered, as I stood marveling over the decorations.

"You always tell me that!" she snapped back. "I wanna speak to *my* daughter, right *now*!" she demanded.

I dropped my smile. I took a deep breath and clutching the phone tightly, I said, "She *really* is asleep. We had a late night last night. I promise, I'll have her call you as soon as she wakes up."

"You're keeping my kids from me! Every time I call they're never around!" she shouted.

Condescendingly, I said, "There's a six-hour time difference, Joan. And it's true; most of the times when you call they're not around because they're up at the pool, or at the beach, or sleeping. I'm not trying to keep them from you." I tried to keep my voice down because I didn't want the kids to wake up.

"You're keeping my kids from me, and I'm not gonna allow you to do that any more!" she yelled back, just before she slammed the phone down.

I pulled the phone away from my ear, and when it came into full view in front of my face, through gritted teeth, I muttered, "You fucking bitch!" With the phone still in my hand, I looked around at everything I had just done to make this a happy, special day for Tessy. It was all I could do to keep myself from throwing the phone through the sliding glass door ten feet away from me. I stood there with my jaw clenched tight and my breathing shallow, steeped in all the heavy feelings of rage and contempt that were familiar to me when dealing with my family. I felt helpless and bitter.

How was it that that brief conversation could trigger such a violent reaction in me? I wanted to bring out the full arsenal of weapons and firearms I had stored inside me. I knew way down deep I resisted wanting and trying to understand my sister's gripes and her point of view. But I didn't want to stay hostage to the animosity and righteous indignation I felt either. I was stuck, wedged in between the familiar bitter resentful feelings and the knowledge that a different approach was available. But I didn't know how to make that shift. I didn't know how to stop the rage inside and forgive, what I believed at that time, to be unforgivable.

Even though I hadn't studied mediation for very long, I had learned ways to manage the little conflicts we all get into from time to time. Though I wasn't practicing them, the tools were in there somewhere, mixed in with all the other artillery. Some of the techniques I had learned were: creating distance from the situation; focused calm breathing; and finding something relaxing, like taking a walk or listening to music, to diffuse the situation at hand. Other interventions included talking (or venting) to a good friend, reframing the mind chatter to something more positive, and oh yeah, practicing forgiveness.

Forgiveness: the ability to let go the need for revenge and
    retribution when wronged or injured.
Forgiveness: to release blame, resentments, upsets and
    negative emotions held against another.
Forgiveness: to liberate the mind and the heart from past
    hurts and failures.
Forgiveness: to pardon another for a grievance against
    yourself.

The morning after Tessy's birthday, Lori left to go back to Northern California and with her went her son, Christopher, and all their friends and family members who had come to visit during the last few weeks. I stood with the kids on the dirt driveway, waving goodbye to everyone as we watched their car turn up the road and vanish out of sight. I turned around and while walking back to the house with Tessy's hand in mine, I realized we were finally alone, just the three of us. It was wonderfully quiet and liberating for the first day or two because we had the entire place to ourselves. But after a couple of days, loneliness crept in, and I found myself facing all my inadequacies. I felt as if a dark hollow cloud had taken up residence in my heart. I felt utterly empty and even scared of myself.

Fear and loneliness are often what is hidden and buried in our bones, when faced with the empty silent moments of our life. Some say loneliness is the absence of love in one's life and heart. The problem for me was, even though I had the kids around me, I still felt the presence of a numbing, lonely existence. It was about that time I remembered a few telephone conversations Joan and I had had over the past year around her breakup with Lilly's father and the loneliness she felt. "But you have three kids to take care of. How can you be lonely?" I remembered asking her.

Alone one evening in Maui, after the kids were tucked in their beds, I lit a candle and sat cross-legged on the floral sofa in the dark, staring at the flickering candlelight shadows on the walls. My thoughts turned toward my sister. My mind slipped to the picture I had taken of her shortly before we left for California. It was a 4 x 5 photo of her sitting on her couch with Timmy on one side of her, Tessy on the other, with Lilly in her lap. It was the last image of her with her family in her house. I had the film developed in Maui. I surprised Tessy for her birthday with that picture in a blue floral frame. Tessy cried, "God's happy tears" when she opened the gift. She held it with both her hands, staring at it adoringly for a long, long time. Smiling, she finally said, "I love it! It's my *bestest* gift of all." She kept that framed picture in her blue quilted backpack, the one her mom had given her and toted it around everywhere she went. At night, she set the picture up on the wicker nightstand next to her bed. When we said our prayers, she always looked over at the picture, talking as if her mommy was right there in the room with us.

Sitting in the long, dark silence, reflecting on Tessy and her affection for that picture and her love for her mother, something shifted. I had a small breakthrough. Just then, the knot that bound me to the fury I felt toward my sister began to loosen. Misty-eyed, I began to sympathize with the loneliness my sister must be feeling and the heartache she must be enduring with the loss of her family and the life she had known and loved. It was the first time I could truly say I felt empathy toward her and her current circumstances.

Maybe I was partly to blame for my sister's reactions and troubles. My inability to forgive her for the way I believed she had encroached on my life was breeding bitterness and resentment. Forgiveness was not just about releasing Joan from the hurt I believed she had caused me. Forgiveness was helping me to free myself from the anger and hatred I felt towards her. Because my resentments were melting a bit, I was able to see that she, like me, was doing the best she could. Even on those days when it didn't seem like it was enough.

# Setbacks

The morning before we left to fly back to California, Dad called.

"Joan's had a setback; she got into a car accident."

"What?" I was shocked. "I thought she wasn't suppose to drive."

"You and I know that. Try telling her that." I could see him in my mind's eye shaking his head in disbelief.

"What happened?" I asked.

"She drove her car to the store to pick up a few groceries. On her way back home, she hit another car."

"So it was her fault?"

"Of course it was!"

"Is she okay? Is she back in the hospital?" I kept my voice lowered, not wanting the kids to overhear me. They were in their bedroom packing.

"No. It wasn't anything *that* serious. She hit her head, but she's okay." He breathed a long, discouraged sigh. He sounded exhausted.

I didn't tell the kids about their mom's accident. Since Joan talked with them every few days, I thought it would be best coming from her.

But there was an even bigger story that day.

Later in the afternoon, the kids and I took a walk by the

cliffs down the road from Lori's house. It had just rained, and I wanted to get a walk in before it got too muggy. Since we were alone at Lori's, I didn't have anyone to watch the kids, so the only option was to take them with me.

"When are we going back, Auntie? This is boring," grumbled Timmy.

"Come on. We agreed, remember? It's important for me to get my walk in every day. Besides, look how beautiful it is here. This is the last time we're going to see this magnificent view of the ocean from the cliffs." I pointed to the deep blue ocean breaking against the rocks below.

"But I wanna go back to the pool. I don't want to walk anymore," he insisted, with his shoulders slumped as he kicked the dirt.

"Yeah, this is stupid. I'm tired. I wanna go back, too," added Tessy.

When I moved to California six years earlier, I started a daily regime of walking and hiking. I loved being in nature, exerting my body, feeling the sweat from the hot sun as I climbed and reached a hilltop or peak. It was like being in the zone for me. Walking and hiking in nature came as naturally as breathing to me. While on the island, since there were so many people at Lori's who kindly offered to watch the kids, I was able to take my daily hikes and was beginning to find my rhythm with it again. As far as I was concerned, there was nothing, absolutely nothing that was going to keep me from getting a walk in on my last day in Maui.

"Auntie, when are we going home?" asked Timmy.

"Yeah, I don't wanna walk any more. I'm tired," moaned Tessy.

As their complaints grew intensely louder, so too did my agitation. We trudged along in single file on the grassy path with me in the lead. At one point, I bent down, grabbed a long tree branch, broke it in half with my knee, and handed each of them a stick.

"Here, this will help. You can use it as a walking stick," I said, then turned around and continued walking.

They were walking like slow pokes. Every twenty or thirty feet, I turned around looking to see how much farther they'd fallen behind. With my Versace's hanging on the tip of my nose, I waved my arm for them to walk faster. "Come on. Let's go," I barked like a drill sergeant giving an order.

Tessy, who was like the little caboose, revolted with an abrupt halt as she threw her stick to the ground. She folded her arms in front of her chest, puckered her lips, wrinkled her nose at me, and yelled, "No! I'm not walking any more. I wanna go back to the pool. And you can't make me go any more."

Faster than a blink of an eye, I turned around, put my hands on my hips, and with a cool eye, I said, "Fine. You can stay right there, all by yourself. I don't care. But when we get back to the pool, you're not going to be allowed to go in." I felt confident I had out smarted her resistance, so I turned back around and continued marching forward.

She threw her hands up into the air and screamed, "Ahhh, I hate you!" before she kicked her stick a few times. Eventually she picked up her stick and resumed her step.

Several moments passed.

"Auntie, when are we going home?" pleaded Timmy.

"It's too hot," moaned Tessy. "I wanna go swimming."

"I'm tired," Timmy moped.

I couldn't stand it any longer. My face grew hot, my neck and head felt as though they were being held in a vise grip. The fire inside me was burning so intensely, I was shaking with rage. I actually had visions of throwing them off the cliff. I began to imagine grabbing hold of each of them and tossing them right over the edge. I stopped marching, turned around toward them, and when they finally arrived and were standing side by side in front of me, I bent over and slapped them each across the face. I hit them just the way my mother used to hit me when I was a little girl. I had hated her for hitting me like that. I had vowed never to do that to a child…not ever.

I stood standing under the blazing hot sun, with my jaw hanging open, stunned, as I watched them both burst into tears. I turned around, away from them, looking out into the vast blue ocean sky and screamed, "*Fuuuck!*" while shaking my tightly fisted hands into the air. There was no way we were going forward with our walk. So we turned around and walked back to the house, with them crying most of the way. Luckily for me, there wasn't anyone around for them to tattle on me. But they didn't have to, because I did a very good job beating myself up for the crime I'd just committed.

An hour later, while sitting on the lounge chair by the pool, watching them swim about, a feeling of shame consumed me. I was afraid the whole world would know the truth: I was nothing more than a mean, ugly, bad person. I thought to myself, *I can't do this any more.* I wanted to call Dad and say, *I give up. This is too difficult. I don't want to be a parent any more.*

Later that night, while helping the kids get ready for bed, I sat on the edge of Tessy's bed and asked the kids to sit down next to me.

With tear filled eyes, I said, "For the last month, every day while you guys have been swimming in the pool, I've been reading books on how to be a better parent. I learned I should teach by example." I lowered my head for a moment and said, "You know how I tell you not to fight and hit?"

"Yesss," they said.

"Well, I learned *I* shouldn't fight or hit either. And I do. Sometimes I fight with your mom or Uncle Steve. And today, I hit you, even though I tell you not to hit each other." I eyed them both back and forth.

"I'm not setting a very good example for you. I'm sorry. You know, even though I'm an adult, I still make mistakes." I hung my head down, feeling so utterly exposed and vulnerable.

Timmy spoke up, "Yeah, it hurt when you hit me." He rubbed his cheek where I had hit him with his hand. "It scared me too."

I looked up at his little face as tears ran down my cheeks and said, "I'm so very sorry. I will try not to do that ever again. I love you both so very much. I'm sorry that I'm bad sometimes."

Tessy, who was wearing her Snow White nightie, was sitting cross-legged next to Timmy. She looked at me sympathetically. Slowly, she reached her little hand over mine and while patting it tenderly, with the eyes of an angel, said, "It's okay, Auntie. Tomorrow will be a better day."

# A Dinner Date

The kids and I arrived in L.A. Since Steve was seeing clients at our home, he thought it best the kids and I stay at my girlfriend Eleanor's house for a couple of nights. She and I met in high school and became fast friends. For almost twenty years we shared, supported, and encouraged each other through the sorrows and triumphs of life. We partied through our college days, stood as bridesmaids for one another, and held each other's hands through our broken marriages. She was the kind of friend whom I could share my deepest, darkest secrets with, though never once did I feel criticized or judged by her. She gave me room to be myself.

Since Eleanor and I had moved to California, we had seen less and less of each other's families, so the kids didn't remember her. Tessy's eyes lit up the moment she met her.

"Oh Auntie, Eleanor's very beautiful," she whispered, while strolling her Pocahontas suitcase into Eleanor's guest bedroom the evening we arrived.

And she was beautiful; she was tall and slender, with big brilliant eyes and sultry lips like Julia Roberts.

The following evening, I was giddy with excitement getting ready for a dinner date with Steve. I felt like a schoolgirl preparing for her prom. It was my first time out without the kids since Joan's stroke. I got all dressed up and wore a pair of sexy tight jeans. I borrowed Eleanor's leopard leather pumps and even put on makeup, something I hadn't done in months.

"What do you think about this top?" I asked Tessy, standing in the bathroom doorway turning from side to side, modeling a Victoria's Secret brown babydoll halter I had borrowed from Eleanor.

"Perfect," she said, nodding her head. "You look very pretty, Auntie."

I even felt pretty, something I hadn't experienced in a long time.

Eleanor took care of the kids for the night. She had a fun evening planned, taking them out for pizza and ice cream, before snuggling in for a movie and popcorn at home. I breathed a sigh of relief feeling safe, knowing I was home again, on familiar ground, surrounded by places and people I trusted and knew well.

Steve and I met at *12 Washington*, a cozy restaurant a block away from the beach in Marina del Rey. We sat across from one another, at a small table with a white linen tablecloth nestled against a bare white stucco wall. He was bathed in an amber glow as the soft candlelight glimmered on his velvety face. We held hands with our eyes attentively fixed upon one another. There was a dull chatter in the room that soon dissolved as we remembered who we were to one another. For a moment, time stood still. I felt wedded and intoxicated by our being together once again. My heart smiled, my eyes welled. The feeling of once again belonging, the touch of my lover, forced my heart to flutter. I felt I was walking on sacred ground again. Steve told me in advance he wanted to talk about the kids and us. I had imagined our talk was to be about our undecided plans. I hoped we would discuss how we'd all live as a family together.

After we ate, Steve sat back in his chair, took a sip of water, breathed a heavy sigh, and said, "I've been so sad the last couple of months watching the distance between us grow. I never told you this, but when I dropped you off at the airport, when you flew back home to be with your family over two months ago, I had an uneasy feeling in my gut that I was going to lose you." He took a lengthy breath. His face was long and serious, his gaze worn.

I could tell he'd been troubled by it all. I hadn't spent much time viewing my life changes through his eyes. In fact, I hadn't wondered about him at all. All my attention, all my focus, had been on my family and our crisis. But now, I could see the effect it had had on him.

He looked at me and with great sadness in his eyes, he said, "I can't tell you I love you and we'll get through all this together. I need to set my boundaries."

I went numb as I quietly listened to him talk, watching his long drawn face and distant gloomy eyes in slow motion, almost like a replay. He talked openly about *his* experience over the last ten weeks. More than once I had a strong urge to interject, ask him questions, but I could see he needed to talk without interruption from me. I saw the dreams we had visioned of our life together fading with his words and the pain and disappointment in his face. My heart ached, as my eyes grew wet.

Then he looked me straight in the eye and said, "I'd like us to explore a non-monogamous relationship."

"A what?" I asked. I leaned forward in a jerk-like movement, placing my folded hands, which were resting on my lap, on top of the table.

"An open relationship," he answered, as he too leaned forward. He then proceeded to plot out our life for the next year. His plan was for the kids and I to live with Lori and Christopher in Northern California. She was fond of the children and eager to help us out. "It's best," he continued, "if you're not in L.A. It'll be too distracting for me. I'll come up to visit you and the kids once a month. After the year's over, after the kids go back to your sister, we can figure out our next step, together." He reached his hand toward mine.

Feeling insulted, I quickly pulled my hands back and placed them on top of my lap. I looked away, staring at another couple smiling while holding hands at a table close by.

With a trembling hand, I reached for the glass of water, took a sip, then looked him in the eyes, and said, "You're kidding me right? This is your idea of setting boundaries? After all I've been through, this is what you want to say to me?"

"All you've been through? What about me? Laura, you've changed. Our relationship has changed," he said. The veins on his neck tightened as his eyes got big and wide.

"How do you expect me to react with all that's been going on?" I asked.

He didn't say anything.

I folded my arms across my chest, then said, "You know, since the very beginning I've never felt your full support. I've felt like I've needed to choose between you and the kids. I get it now, my struggle is with *you*, not the kids."

"You didn't even consult me about taking the kids. You just called me up and told me you were taking them. How do you expect *me* to react?" He tapped his index finger forcefully on the table a couple of times.

"What was I suppose to do? Let them go into foster homes? They're my family! They need me!"

"You're angry all the time. We're not getting along," he insisted.

"I'm stressed out! I've been in a huge crisis, as you so pointed out. I need support, not someone telling me he's not getting his sexual needs met and wants to have an affair."

"Not an affair," he retorted, as he leaned back in his chair and folded his arms in front of his chest.

There was a short pause.

"It doesn't really matter any more," I said. "As far as I'm concerned, we can call this relationship over, as of now. You're free to do as you please, with whomever you choose." I smiled at him contemptuously.

I grabbed my leather purse strap that was hanging on the corner of my chair and placed my purse on top of my lap. I inched my way to the edge of my seat.

"You're breaking us up?" His body jolted forward. He sat upright in his chair. He looked surprised, even offended.

"I don't see it that way. You're the one who broke us up. I don't need this. And I don't need you. I've got enough on my plate."

In the long run, I figured it would be a lot easier for me to raise the kids without him. Maybe it was pride, maybe I had known the truth since our nightly conversations back at Joan's house, but hadn't wanted to give voice to it. It was clear, I no longer held first place in my lover's heart, and I wasn't about to settle for anything less.

I stormed out of the restaurant and headed straight for the beach. The warm muggy night air was almost still. The salty smell of the ocean, the sounds of crashing waves, reminded me how I had longed to be back home in California. Finally, here I was, walking under the silver moon, on the same beach Steve and I had walked on so many nights before. But I hadn't imagined being back on the beach this way.

Rage burned inside me as I revisited our breakup scene over and over again in my head. I couldn't cry. I didn't understand why. I'd never given myself to a man the way I had to Steve. I'd never shared love in the way I had with him. Yet, I was unable to shed a tear. My body felt tight and rigid, my mind was consumed with sneering thoughts about how wronged I felt by him.

What had given me pause to feelings of being so offended, were his words, "You yell a lot, you're tired all the time, you're always in a hurry, and we don't make love like we used to. I don't know who you are anymore. And I don't like being around you. You're angry and stressed, all the time. I'm seeing a part of you that scares the hell out of me." For a moment it hit me and made me wonder, *had I become a scornful woman like my mother?*

# Family Camp

I woke the following morning expecting to feel heartbroken or at least gloomy, but instead, I felt lighter, free from the inside. I opened my eyes and saw the bright blue L.A. skies outside the bedroom window. The song of birds in the full-bloomed violet Jacaranda tree made me smile. With fresh eyes, I knew it was time to move forward and find *our* place in the world.

After Eleanor left for work, I sat at the breakfast table with the kids. While spreading jam on my English muffin, I said, as casually as I could, "Uncle Steve and I had dinner together last night. We've decided not to get married and we're not together anymore."

Tessy, who had just placed a spoonful of cereal into her mouth, quickly looked up at me and said, "Will he still be our uncle?" as milk dribbled from the corner of her mouth.

"Sure. He'll still be your uncle. But he won't be in your life every day like me," I said, reaching for the almond butter. "And please, don't talk with your mouth full."

"Oops," she said, smirking as she covered her mouth with her hand.

"When will we see him again?" asked Timmy. "Uncle Steve *promised* he'd take me to a Dodgers' game."

Timmy had a vested interest in maintaining contact with

Steve. He liked Steve, a lot. Their relationship had begun when Steve took him to a Red Sox game the previous summer. They came back wearing matching navy blue caps with an embroidered red "B'" on the front. They spent hours together watching televised baseball games in Joan's living room, with Steve lying on the couch and Timmy stretched out on the floor. They cheered and booed, while sharing commentary on the scoring and competency of the players. Steve *had* promised to take Timmy to a Dodger's game, and Timmy often reminded him of his promise. I knew it wouldn't be the same if I offered to take him, because, as Timmy pointed out, "Sometimes guys gotta do guy stuff by themselves."

"I'm sure Uncle Steve will keep his promise. It won't be right now because we're leaving to go camping. Remember?" I nodded.

"Oh yeah, dang, I forgot. But next time you talk to Uncle Steve, can you make sure he remembers that he *promised* to take me to a game?"

And that was it. Much to my surprise, our conversation moved along to other matters. Our breakup didn't seem to have much of an effect on them. I was greatly relieved.

Later that morning we drove to Steve's house. The kids swam in the pool while I repacked and off we went. By early afternoon, we were on the 101 Freeway heading north. Lori had invited us to join her and Christopher camping in the Sierras for ten days. It wasn't just ordinary camping; it was a progressive "family camp" program run by two developmental psychologists and a team of family counselors. The program's aim was to teach families how to communicate and work in collaboration with each other. Timmy and Tessy didn't care much about the structure of the program. They were only interested in the fun they'd have camping on the river with lots of other kids.

I felt it was important to go, even though my mission was to find us a home before school started in September. We had less than a month. I didn't have anything keeping me in L.A. any longer. I didn't know where we were going, but since Steve and I were no longer in relationship, it gave me the green light to move forward, to be in the mystery and the unfolding of life with the kids. I didn't have a clue what our life together was going to look like. I was scared, but in some way I wasn't. I felt as if I were in a void of some kind, not knowing the particulars of how things were going to work out. Mostly I knew I needed to keep moving forward and since we had already made arrangements weeks before to attend the camp with Lori, it seemed like the next right thing to do.

We spent a couple of days in Marin at Lori's house before heading to Pathfinder's Camp. We followed behind Lori in my Camry wagon for the three-hour drive. Upon our arrival, Lori introduced the kids and I to Ba and Josette Luvmour, the founders of the program. Ba handed me their book, *Natural Learning Rhythms,* and suggested I start reading it right away so I would understand the basics of their program.

The kids and I spent the next ten days working as a team. Jointly we set up the five-person tent we had borrowed from Lori. Then we rolled out our mats and sleeping bags, more equipment on loan from Lori. Next we organized our clothes in piles and we used Timmy's Red Sox backpack to store our toiletries in. Three times a day we lined up along long metal tables, cafeteria style, for meals prepared by staff. We ate as a family with other families. There were approximately thirty other children ranging in age from five to sixteen. Our days were packed with team-building exercises like a rope course, a river rafting expedition, cooperative games and activities, and one-on-one parenting counseling sessions.

On our first morning, the kids and I met Peggy, our team counselor, at the Big Trees post. It was our designated meeting spot where we gathered daily for instructions on a different team-building exercise.

"Now, we call this exercise the Blindfold Trust Walk," said Peggy, as she handed each of us a blue nylon blindfold with a thick black stretch band. "Can you guess what we're going to do?"

Timmy placed the blindfold on top of his head. "Yeah, I know." He raised his hand in the air. "We're gonna put these blindfolds on, and we're gonna help each other walk around without bumping into anything," he said, with the confidence of someone who had experience.

"Very good, Timmy," she replied. Peggy then pointed to a shady cluster of oak trees across the fire road. "You see those woods over there?" After we nodded, she continued, "Well, after you put your blindfolds on, I'm going to take your Aunt Laura's hand and lead her through the small narrow trail over by the sign post. And she's going to hold your hand, Tessy, and Tessy's going to hold your hand, Timmy. You're going to talk to one another and help each other around turns and over fallen tree branches along the path."

We spent the next hour helping each other, while stumbling and tripping, find our way along the wooded paths.

Every day was an unexpected adventure of learning how to communicate and trust one another. Tessy got really scared when it came her turn to climb forty feet up a pine tree for her first rope course experience. Burt, a college student junior counselor, strapped a light blue high-strength polyester webbing harness around her legs and chest. It was attached to a heavy rope that her climbing partner, Karen, another junior counselor, maneuvered from the ground below. With a school bus yellow helmet strapped on her head, Tessy timidly climbed the iron footing along the tree. The whole way, Timmy, who was standing next to me on the ground, coaxed her by saying, "You can do it, Tessy! Don't look down. You're almost there. You're doing great!" When she reached the top wooden platform, Karen hooked her into a zip line, and down she flew with great ease.

During the afternoons, the kids played cooperative games designed to build social skills. In the evenings, we toasted marshmallow s'mores on long sticks, sang songs around the campfire, and listened to storytellers narrate imaginative, compelling tales. On our last evening at the camp, all the kids performed a theatrical piece demonstrating the many ways people work together to help one another and the problems that can arise when they don't.

Timmy was a natural in his role. He played a camp counselor and wore a silver whistle on a black cord around his neck and a red baseball cap that read "Camp Counselor." On stage, he explained to two new campers—that's what they called us, "campers"—how to work together in a two-person potato-sack race. As he demonstrated with another actor how to jump in the brown burlap sack together, they both fell on the stage. Everyone in the audience, including Timmy and all the kids in the performance, laughed and laughed.

While reading *Natural Learning Rhythms* and working with the counselors, I was learning valuable new parenting skills, which helped me to build confidence in my ability to care for the kids' needs, rather than always feeling I was in a reactive state trying to manage problems and complaints. Ba explained to me that Timmy and Tessy resided in the first stage of their model, Body Being.

"The Body Being Stage," he explained, "focuses primarily on body sensations. When the kids are having a difficult moment, it isn't your responsibility to make them feel better.

Your job is to be present with them. Standing by them in their experience is enough. It's not necessary to try to 'fix them' or 'make them happy.' "They need to have their own feelings and be allowed to express themselves fully in those feelings."

I had the occasion to practice this new technique one day when Timmy came barreling down the hillside while I was talking with another parent.

He came up to me panting and said, "Auntie, can I go down to the swimming hole with the other kids? They're leaving now. I wanna go. Can I? *Please*?" He was bouncing with excitement, his arms squirming like an eel by his side.

"Not now, maybe later. We have a counseling session soon," I told him and turned back to resume my conversation.

"But *all* the other kids are going. *Please*," he pleaded, inching his chin forward, straining his neck as he clasped his fingers tightly together in prayer in front of his chest.

"I hear you want to go with the other kids. You can join them *after* we're done with our session."

He stomped his feet and then added, "But, it's not fair!"

I squatted halfway down, becoming eye level with him and said, "I understand."

"But, but all the other kids are going," he ranted, as he swung his arms up into the air.

"I hear you," I said, while nodding my head.

"But I want to go!" he yelled, thrusting his arms down at his side.

Again, I nodded my head, letting him know I had heard him. I didn't try to convince him to see things my way, nor did I try to make him feel other than what he was feeling. I stood there watching him have the full expression of his experience.

"But it's not fair!" he wailed again.

Eventually he stopped whining. Sure, he walked away

disgruntled, with his head hung low, kicking the ground as he made his way back to the other kids, muttering how "unfair" it was. But twenty minutes later, when we joined together for our daily counseling session, he was fine.

Family camp was in some ways a rest stop for me. Timmy and Tessy got along great and as a result, I didn't need to do so much conflict control. Their focus and attention was mostly on playing with other kids. Since there was plenty of supervision, I didn't feel like I needed to watch them all the time.

One day while standing on the side of the fire road under a shady tree, I had a good view of the kids in the meadow playing games led by the junior counselors.

Our team counselor Peggy, walked up behind me, put her arm around my shoulder, and said, "Just watch them. You'll learn a lot about them if you just stand back and observe their behaviors from a distance."

I wondered why Tessy sat with the young teenage girls, rather than girls her own age. I saw Timmy, who was playing on the boys' side of the meadow, take charge of a situation when a young boy was having a difficult time. When Timmy saw one of his team members sitting on the picnic table by himself crying, Timmy waved his arms to everyone, like someone flagging down a car and said, "Hey, everyone, time out." Then he formed a "T" with both his hands and added, "Jordan's sitting at the picnic table and he's upset. We need to help Jordan out."

I was also able to get some much-desired alone time. As a result, I had the chance to take long hikes every day on my own. I felt rejuvenated by having that precious time. I actually felt like there really was a God listening to my needs after all. So while on my walks, I started a practice of having conversations with God. I vented my worries and concerns and voiced my grievances. In my solitude, I even released big tears over my breakup with Steve.

As I hiked, losing myself in the steep rugged canyons of dense oaks while wandering alongside the wild rushing river below, I became absorbed in the majesty of the natural world. The terrain was new for me, yet it felt ancient, even mystical in some way. Amongst the trees, I felt intensely aware of something greater than myself and found myself repeating, *Everything's going to work out.* What's more, I actually believed what I was telling myself.

## Finding Home

We followed Lori and Christopher back to Marin. I accepted play dates for the kids as I looked for signs for our next move. I checked out a few housing opportunities, attended a networking party with Lori, and looked into job prospects in hopes that something would call to me. In the meantime, the kids and I had fun with local activities such as The Discovery Museum, nature walks, and rollerblading along the San Francisco Bay. We took a day trip to Pier 39, where the kids had a blast performing aerial acrobatics on a twenty-foot bungee trampoline. We visited the boisterous barking sea lions and were captivated by a handful of street performers: talented jugglers, a teary-eyed mime dressed as a hobo, and a gold metallic man who stood as still as stone—even I thought he was a statue. He fooled Timmy though. In his hand he held a crisp one-dollar bill.

"Look you guys, free money," yelled Timmy, as he ran up to the man and tried to yank the bill out of his hand. The performer quickly bent over, grabbed hold of Timmy's wrist, and retrieved his money faster than Timmy knew what was happening to him. Timmy was stunned. "Ahhh! Auntie!" he yelped, his eyes looking like they were about to bulge out of their sockets.

Tessy and I stood hand in hand next to the parking meter,

laughing and pointing at him. Seconds later he too burst into a roaring belly laugh. We talked and chuckled about that performer—and Timmy's reaction—for days to come.

Even though I was a bit worried, unsure where the kids and I belonged, I never felt a bleak moment. I stayed focused on tending to their daily needs, while persistently practicing my new mantra on my daily solo walks: *Everything's going to work out.* By now the children were beginning to burrow their way further into my heart. I wanted nothing more than to love and care for them in the best possible way. With fierce faith and velocity in my step, I prayed for help, guidance, and a home.

Back in Los Angeles, my girlfriend Shirley had been checking out schools for the kids, just in case things up north didn't work out for us. And things didn't fall into place for us in Marin. Lori graciously invited us to live with her and Christopher, but Timmy and Christopher didn't really get along. Christopher spent hours in the media room, in front of his big screen TV playing video games. He was good at them. So was Timmy. But whenever Timmy and Tessy walked into the room, Christopher would ask, "Do you want to play, Tessy?"

"Nah," she'd say, finding something else to amuse herself with.

But he never invited Timmy to join in on a game with him. I didn't understand why. When I asked Timmy about it, he just shrugged his shoulders and muttered, "I don't know."

I didn't want to press the issue. But as time went on, the boy's distance grew. It was painful for me to watch Timmy sitting on the couch saying, "I'll play with you," when most times Christopher just ignored him. Although I didn't want to live in L.A., I was running out of options. The kids needed to be in school in a week's time. We had no other choice but to drive back to Los Angeles, where I had friends who I knew would help me piece our life together.

The day before we left Lori's house, I called Wendy and Michael, Lori's sister and brother-in-law. The kids had had a fun time playing with Michael's daughter, Briana, during their stay in Maui. Michael had invited us to spend a day or two at their home in Santa Cruz whenever we were in the area.

Briana was a sweet, gentle, kind-hearted kid. She had a strong affection toward animals and had taken to the water like a fish. You couldn't miss her; she wore a cobalt blue one-piece bathing suit with bold yellow and orange tropic fish and a ruffled skirt. She approached life slowly, though was fearless riding the waves on her boogie board.

We arrived at their home somewhere around three in the afternoon. They lived two miles up a private, winding, twisting, and turning road, past a gated entrance, through a dense growth of redwoods and pines, in the Santa Cruz Mountains. The kids and I trotted up the thirty-step mauve granite walkway, arriving at a spacious, elegant main entrance. To the left of the massive custom leaded glass door was a multi-tiered waterfall with rose quartz inlays that spilled into a pond filled with tropical yellow and black striped fish. Bougainvillea, both red and pink, burst up the sidewall on an arched trellis with green native foliage below. To the right stood a six-foot bronze Zen bell.

Tessy dropped to her knees, picked up a blue stone from the garden walkway, and said, "Auntie, I've never seen a blue rock before. This is *so* beautiful. Can I keep it? *Please*?"

Within seconds Michael answered the door. He was a person of great heart. With a gleam in his eyes and a sweeping open palm, he greeted us, "You made it! Welcome!"

He was a tall, muscular man, strikingly handsome with

a mustache and goatee, wearing khaki shorts and a blue Hawaiian short-sleeved silk shirt. Briana stood next to him with a bright yellow Lion King beach towel draped over her shoulders. She was quiet, even shy as she stood watching us enter into the foyer, with her arm wrapped around her dad's leg. She didn't greet us right away. Instead, she turned to her dad and said, "Daddy, can Timmy and Tessy come into the pool with me?"

"Sure. Let's ask them."

Michael bent down low, placed his hands on his knees, and asked, "You kids want to go into the pool?"

"Yeah!" they yelled, looking at each other then up at me.

"Can we, Auntie? Can we go swimming with Briana?"

"Sure," I nodded and followed the children as they pranced their way up the wide stairway.

Antique bronze deities and European marble statues were stunningly displayed on cream and gold limestone landings along both sides of the staircase. I was mesmerized by the sprawling elegance of fine Asian carved furnishings, oriental rugs, and silk wall tapestries, as we made our way through the main hallway out onto the granite patio.

Within moments, the kids were splashing and giggling in the swimming pool, diving off the massive jump stone used instead of a diving board. A blue tiled in-ground Jacuzzi rested fifteen feet away, surrounded by native California foliage of white sage, with lavender wisteria vines climbing a thin white wood lattice behind a stunning rock garden waterfall. I could see endless acres of green treetops below, stretching before us until they met the sparkling blue bay waters far off in the distance. I felt as if I were on top of the world.

I sat at the oval tempered glass patio table, under the shady blue oak tree, getting reacquainted with Michael. He was an artist and political activist. He appreciated beauty and fine art and had a sense of passion in all his actions and speech.

"Where was this taken?" I asked, pointing to a framed image of an ancient white monastery perched on a hillside above a valley, with tattered prayer flags fluttering in the wind.

"That's Taktsang Monastery in Bhutan. It's also known as the Tiger's Nest. The Bhutanese people are some of the finest in the world. They're incredibly sweet. It's their tradition to honor every guest with great hospitality. I spent a month trekking through their sacred land last year."

I felt somewhat inadequate, shying away from the conversation. I'd never heard of Bhutan and didn't know what trekking meant. It was evident he spent most of his life traveling the world, where he acquired beautiful artifacts and poignant stories of places and people.

Wendy arrived home later that afternoon. As the light gave way to evening darkness, we all joined together in the dining room for dinner. Michael sat at the head of the table, Wendy to his right, Briana to his left. I sat at the other end with Timmy and Tessy on each side of me. Together we gabbed for a while, sharing informal conversation.

At one point, Timmy looked over at me while picking away at his chicken drumstick and asked politely, "Auntie, can we live *here*? We like it here. This is a fun house, and I really like Briana, don't you?"

With my breath held, I blushed in embarrassment and forced a grin. "Yes, Timmy, Briana is very nice. You know we're leaving tomorrow to drive back down to L.A. Remember?" I flipped him a weak smile.

"Oh, yeah. Dang. I forgot." He continued, "but I really like it here."

With shy eyes, I glanced over at Michael. He caught my

eye and with a wink, he smiled. I grinned bashfully, steering my gaze away from him.

Later that evening, after I tucked the kids into bed, I walked into my bedroom, which was located next to the kid's bedroom. We were in the east wing of the house, which partially consisted of two bedrooms, a private bathroom off my bedroom, and a bathroom outside the room the kids slept in. I walked into my bathroom and turned on the tub water so I could take a bath. I heard a knock on the door and hurried to open it. Wendy and Michael stood in the hallway, arm in arm. I stepped back, inviting them into the room.

"Are you finding everything okay?" asked Michael, stepping into the room, holding Wendy's hand in his. They were both about ten years older than I and had been together only a couple of years.

"Yeah, thank you. The kids are in bed. I was just running a tub. Let me shut it off." I dashed out of the room quickly and returned. The three of us stood standing in the middle of the bedroom.

"You know, Laura, I spoke with Ba yesterday after your call," said Michael, placing his arm around Wendy's waist.

I interrupted him, "I didn't know you knew Ba." I eyed both of them back and forth.

"Yeah, we've been to family camp ourselves. They're good people and have a great program." Wendy smiled and shook her head in agreement.

"Ba spoke highly of your dedication and efforts to care for your sister's children. We're aware of the situation you're in."

He paused.

"We also know about your recent breakup with Steve."

It was an awkward moment for me. I tucked my head slightly down, my cheeks flushed; feeling a bit self-conscious—

or maybe it was a feeling of being exposed. It was through Steve I had come to know Lori and now Wendy and Michael. I hadn't talked with Steve since that night at the restaurant. I wasn't sure how or what they had heard about our breakup.

"You know, Wendy and I built this home not just for ourselves, but with the intention of sharing it, living communally. We just completed construction this spring and no one has lived here with us yet." He turned his gaze to Wendy. They looked adoringly into each other's eyes, then back at me.

"We'd like to help you and the kids out. Your service to your family is admirable. You have a couple of great kids. It's wonderful to see them all get along so well. When we arrived home from Maui, Briana talked a great deal about the kids."

A polite silence filled the room.

"Thanks. I think they're great kids, too," I said with a shy smile.

"Wendy and I have been talking about this, and we would like to invite you and the kids to live here with us. We understand your plan is to take the kids back to your sister next summer. You can live here, in this wing of the house, until then. We don't really use it. There's a local elementary school four miles down the road. You can enroll the kids right away, and they can start school next week. You'd have to drive them to and from school everyday, of course, because we live on a private road and there's no bus service that comes up this way."

Tears of gratitude welled in my eyes. I couldn't believe our good fortune. I could hear the rapid thumping of my own heartbeat and like lightning through clouds, my heart leaped as I exhaled a huge sigh of relief.

Not long afterwards, I lay soaking in the tub, with a crescent moon shimmering outside the bathroom window. I relaxed as I listened to the tune of crickets against the warm muggy night air. The sweet smell of summer grasses lingered as I let my mind softly dream. I remembered something Michael Beckwith at the Agape International Spiritual Center, once said, "If we keep our mindsets and heart-sets on what is positive in this world, we will see the good in every person and circumstance in our life. We will experience our interactions with others as blessings. So set your heart and mind upon that which is inspiring and uplifting."

What amazed me was not the wealth Wendy and Michael lived in, but the kindness in the world, the generosity of hearts that had been extended our way. My small mind couldn't fully comprehend the gift of being so cared and provided for. In a moment of divine silence, what arose was a belief or faith in the process and unfolding of life. I believed God to be smiling over us and felt a sense of homecoming I'd never known before.

# Motherhood

The kids jumped around elatedly, screaming, "Yippee!" when I told them the news. They spent the next week splashing around in the pool with their new best friend, Briana. We had more than just a roof over our heads. The detached three-car garage had been turned into a little schoolhouse, complete with desks for eight kids. There was a small two-bedroom house on the property, plus a two-story tree house, a tennis court, and a wildflower meadow with a yurt and a tetherball.

The house contained a gym, a sauna, a Kiva, two outdoor showers, and an enormous granite patio that housed silver tricycles and an antique hanging Balinese wooden garden swing. Located in the west wing of the house were an art studio, a guest bedroom, two bathrooms, and a huge gathering room complete with a full kitchen.

Most evenings we lounged in the family room on the oversized teal green sofa and chair, with a huge steel bowl of buttered popcorn, watching movies on the big-screen TV. The family room was actually a multi-media room with technology that took me months to learn. But the kids picked it up fast. Within days they knew how to eject the silver screen from the ceiling and turn the music on outside by the pool.

Included in our new extended family portrait were

Briana's longhaired golden retriever, Sashi, and Wendy's barking Pomeranian, Shanti. Michael's ex-wife, Susan, lived in the separate two-bedroom house, offering a convenient way to co-parent their daughter, Briana. Since we hardly knew one another, we all gathered in the main living room twice a month to discuss the overall comfort of our living situation. We divided up job responsibilities. It was Tessy's job at the end of every day to make sure all the floats and toys were out of the pool and stacked neatly in the wooden pool shed. Timmy had the task of hanging all the towels on the railings and to make sure the patio was unobstructed by toys and games.

Within days we were introduced to all the people who helped mange the household: white uniformed housekeepers, a cook, gardeners, maintenance staff, secretaries, and business associates. We learned a different way of living; we made agreements rather than rules, emphasizing each person's voice being heard. A couple of times a week we all gathered for big family dinners. The three kids set the table while we adults took turns cooking. Everyone helped clean up before dessert was served. Since Wendy and Michael traveled almost half the year, giving the kids and I lots of opportunity to be together privately, to bond, and to heal ourselves from the trauma we'd been through.

Both Joan and Dad were delighted to hear our news. Since the kids and I were now homed, Joan had easy access to her children. Care packages and cards arrived almost weekly from her. Everyday when I picked the kids up from school, with hope and anticipation, they asked, "Did we get anything from Mom today?" It didn't matter what they received, it was all the same to them; they marveled over every card, as well as the toys, clothes, and trinkets she sent them.

Dad and I found an easeful rhythm checking in every Wednesday morning after I returned home from dropping the kids off at school. It was our time to talk in depth about the day-to-day events in our independent, yet collective lives.

One afternoon after Michael and Timmy returned from running errands in Michael's Porsche Carrera, Timmy skipped into the kitchen while I was flipping grilled cheese sandwiches and asked, "Are we rich, Auntie?"

I turned around with the spatula in my hand and replied, "Michael and Wendy are financially wealthy. We, my dear, are rich in spirit." I was now convinced of the presence of invisible guiding hands supporting us through our daily existence.

But the challenges of parenthood were many.

While sitting at the breakfast table before school one morning, Timmy asked, "Can I have some more orange juice?" after guzzling the glass I'd just poured him.

"Sorry, honey, we're out," I said, poking my head in the refrigerator.

"What? That's not fair! I want more juice!" he demanded, as he pushed his cereal bowl away, spilling milk all over the table. He kicked his feet under his chair, hammered his fists on top of the table, squeezed his eyes shut, and began to cry.

"Come on, Timmy. You just spilt milk *all* over the table. Stop it now. You're too big to be crying like that," I said sharply, looking for a towel to clean up the mess.

Then I stopped myself, and while watching him in his reaction, I realized his tears were real. It dawned on me that his cries might not necessarily be about the OJ. I thought maybe his tears were about his pain, his fear, or his loss. Maybe in that moment, he was expressing the difficulty life can sometimes be for any of us. Then I remembered it wasn't about me scolding him or trying to make it better for him. I needed to just let him have his own experience and be there to listen and support him.

Then I thought, as I felt a hollow, sadness from within, *I don't even do that for myself. How am I going to do that for the kids?*

A few days later, while eating a salad on the patio and chatting with Michael, I watched Tessy climb out of the pool, wrap herself in her purple Pocahontas beach towel, and crawl like a two-year old into my lap. She stuck her thumb into her mouth and began sucking it like an infant. I cradled and rocked her in my arms, gently stroking the top of her hair, occasionally leaning over to kiss her forehead and cheeks.

"Goo goo gaga," she repeated, over and over again, gazing longingly upon me, all the time curled in a fetal position, sucking her thumb.

"Oh, my beautiful baby," I said softly, my heart warmed like the sun. "You're such a good little baby girl. I love my baby. My baby makes me so happy," I murmured affectionately, in between coos and caresses.

After a few moments, she jumped up out of my arms, sashaying contentedly over toward Timmy and Briana, who were sitting on the jump stone trying to fix a broken walkie-talkie. I wasn't sure what to make of her infantile gestures. They happened frequently. Intuitively I sensed she needed some form of nurturing, and I enjoyed giving it to her. I liked the feeling of caring and mothering a vulnerable little one. It made me feel needed and wanted, in a delicate way.

Attention on the both of them was needed constantly; it was a full time job. I was forever dropping my agenda to tend to their needs, sharing in their triumphs, managing their complaints, and being there for everything else in-between.

One day after school while I was making lemonade, Tessy came into the kitchen from the patio crying and said, "Auntie, Timmy threw my yellow noodle over the railing."

"I'll be out in a minute," I said, grabbing glasses out of the cabinet.

Moments later when I reappeared on the patio, she was standing on the jump stone giggling as she watched Timmy whacking the water with his arms, bobbing his head up and down, and making "zzzzzzz" sounds into the air between gasps of breath, as he pretended to gag and choke. He was trying to imitate a drowning bug.

I was surprised to see how "in the moment" they were. I'd been learning, as part of my meditation studies over the past year or so, the importance of being in the moment. Though I must admit, I'd been trying to understand it from an intellectual perspective. Here, every moment of each day, the kids were displaying it to me in action. It was all a mixed bag of raw, dramatic emotions and feelings—anger, sadness, excitement, and joy. I felt alive from it all, realizing I was living more fully. Every day was a new experience; I felt engaged with life in a newfound way.

I remember back in L.A., while sitting with co-workers in the lunchroom, how oftentimes the topic of conversation turned to motherhood. "Anyone can be a mother. It takes a special person to run an accounting department," was often my response to the discussion. Boy, was that a line of bullshit now. For the first time I was able to get a glimpse into the fear, or ambivalence, or maybe it was just plain confusion I had wrapped around the idea of motherhood.

When I was in my mid-twenties, while having dinner with my husband Billy at our favorite restaurant one evening, I told him, "I have everything I could possibly want—you, a beautiful home, a career I'm passionate about, great friends, plenty of money in the bank. But, I feel, I feel so empty on the inside."

"Have a baby," was his response, "then you'll have

something to fill your life with."

But that never felt like the right answer for me.

I didn't explore motherhood with Billy. I could only guess it was a timing issue; my career had been my priority. But living as a family with Timmy and Tessy, I was beginning to see my fear and ambivalence and confusion had been in my attachment to my identity. I had measured my worth based on an idea of success I had envisioned in my head, rather than the reverence and compassion of touching the soul of another human being.

# Nourishment

I'd been a practicing vegan for the past three years, which meant I didn't eat animal products like meat, dairy, or eggs. Since the kids had been in my care, for the most part, I had made them adhere to my diet, preferring they ate vegetarian-based foods. They hated my diet. They loved sitting down to dinner with Wendy, Michael, and the gang, because everyone ate a lot of chicken, which I didn't protest. Mostly we ate fish and of course lots of vegetables and rice. I wasn't fond of them eating hamburgers and hotdogs.

Tessy often voiced how "stupid" my diet restrictions were. She *loved* hotdogs; they were her favorite food. I tried to get her to eat tofu dogs, but the only time she did, she took one bite, spit it onto her plate, and complained, "That's gross!" Disgust was written all over her face, as if I had just made her eat a dead rat. She refused my attempts to get her to try another bite ever again.

Wednesday afternoons became our weekly grocery shopping time. I'd pick the kids up at school and drive to downtown Santa Cruz. First we'd go to the farmer's market, where the kids stood mesmerized watching Mr. Twister, the local clown, make balloon animals for an audience of both children and adults. Then we'd walk around the corner to New Leaf, the local health food store. I let the kids go off on their own for a few minutes in the store so I could have some breathing space, because most of the time while I read food labels and tried to make my mind up about buying particular foods, they'd hang around asking, "Are you done yet?" "When are we leaving?" "I'm bored." I also thought letting them wander was a way to give them a small taste of independence.

Tessy never stayed away too long. Moments after she and Timmy took off to check out the candy display or ice cream section, she'd peer down each aisle in desperate search for me, looking a bit fraught. Once she found me, she'd walk up to me saying, in her smallest, most vulnerable voice, "I missed you, Auntie. I was sad being without you," as she slipped her tiny hand into mine.

"I missed you too, Princess," I'd say, as I bowed down, kissing the top of her head, stroking her hair, squeezing her gently close to me. She touched me deeply and made me know soft love. Her vulnerability, the way she needed me, made my heart swell.

Timmy was a different story. He was the one who needed, even insisted on having his independence. "I need time away from being with *girls* all the time," he sulked every so often. While sitting at the dinner table one evening, Timmy turned to Michael and said, "I like living here with you Michael. You and me are the only guys in the house. When I lived back in Brockton, I lived with my mom and two sisters. It wasn't fair to live with just *girls* all the time." It made a difference for Timmy to have even a little bit of freedom; he was just easier to be around.

While walking down the cereal aisle one September Wednesday afternoon, I glanced up and saw Timmy hanging around the meat counter; the way kids hang around candy displays. He was eyeing the meat selection with great focus, with his tongue hanging out the side of his mouth. He moved closer to the meat counter and then pressed his lips up against the giant glass, which fogged around his face as he breathed deeply. His arms were stretched above his head, with his hands resting on top of the stainless steel counter. I chuckled, shook my head amusingly, and continued shopping.

Moments later, in a loud high-pitched voice, with his lips still pressed against the glass, he roared, "Auntie, I *need* meat! *M-e-a-t*! I *need meat,* Auntie!"

Startled, I rushed to the end of the aisle to get a view of what was going on. He stood pinned to the glass, with his arms still stretched above his head holding onto the countertop, with his forehead slightly pounding the glass above the red meat section. A couple of senior women wearing matching lemon-yellow sun visors were standing behind him with deli tickets in their hands. They looked at each other, shook their heads, and broke out into a laughter. But the moment I heard Timmy's wail, I realized the truth—my vegan diet wasn't necessarily *his* thing. With Tessy's hand mine, we strolled up behind him. I placed the food basket on the floor, gave Tessy a wink, and placed both my hands on top of Timmy's shoulders. With his eyes still fixated on the meat, I leaned into him and asked, "Do you want a steak, Timmy?"

"Yeah, yeah, yeah!" he said, with the eyes of a drunken poet, his tongue hanging out over his lower lip like a dog waiting for a bone.

On the drive back home, we had an open discussion about the meat issue. "We're kids, and we like going to McDonald's," said Timmy, peering up from his Game Boy.

"Okay, I get it now. I'm sorry. I'm an inexperienced parent, and I make mistakes. So, how about we go to McDonald's once a week? Does that work for you guys?"

With my hands on the steering wheel, I shot him a glance in the rearview mirror. Tessy, who was sitting in the front seat, immediately turned around to look at Timmy. They both nodded in agreement, high-fived each other, and then clapped their hands.

I was reminded of a conversation I had had with Wendy only days before. She said, "The kids will know. Just watch and listen to them. They know what they want and need." I didn't have a clue what she was talking about. But on the drive home, I thought, *Maybe this was one of those revealing moments. Maybe this was a way they informed me what they needed.* Though she had never had children of her own, Wendy had the motherly wisdom of a great elder. She had been raised in affluence and moved with a quiet grace, much like a queen. Mostly she was a gentle, loving, kind-hearted person.

The following day, while the children were in school, Wendy invited me to attend an art class with her. It was a six-week series that met Thursday mornings for three hours. The class was just beginning; I jumped at her invitation.

I was entranced the moment I set foot into the art studio, a converted two-car garage. The room smelled of paint and freshly sharpened pencils. The cement floor was splattered with paint in every hue, and the plaster walls were the colors of a sunset. Two huge, thick wooden tables were joined together in the center of the room. Together we were eight women sitting on wooden barstools around the tables. I immediately felt opened from the inside, at home, while at the same time overflowing with exhilaration and wonderment…I was finally in an art class.

Judy, our teacher, had long black shimmering hair reaching past her waist. She wore black stretch pants, denim Keds covered with paint, and a worn long-sleeved floral periwinkle cotton pocket smock. The metal rim around her eyeglasses was aqua in color. She wore long Native American turquoise and white beaded brick-stitch earrings that almost touched her shoulders. She looked like an artist.

She addressed us first by saying, "Art expresses what language cannot." I hung on to every word she uttered thereafter. Following introductions, she passed out thick white drawing paper and small wicker baskets brimming with brightly colored pencils, markers, crayons, and pastels. I immediately went to work drawing the same yellow brick road I had colored when I was in fourth grade, over again and again.

I had drawn a scene from *The Wizard of Oz* in pastels for the school art fair. I'd been working on it for weeks. While putting the final touches on my drawing, I messed up—while thickening the lines on the yellow brick road, I made a huge, thick, black blotch down the center of the picture. It was too late for me to recreate the piece. I had to enter it just as it was. Surprisingly, I won honorable mention. But I hung my head in disappointment when the nun announced, "Sandra Leanous takes first prize with her picture titled, *Flower Bouquet*." Sandra was my close friend, and she had used the same pastels I used. When she finished her art piece, our art teacher, Mrs. Shadley, sprayed her artwork with a shiny coating, giving it an extra gloss. It was stunningly beautiful! Every flower was a perfect burst of perfumed joy. I was embarrassed with my artwork. All I could see was that big, black, ugly blotch.

Weeks later when we received our art pieces back, I tore mine up on the way home from school. I placed it in the neighbor's tin trashcan, tucking it deep inside so no one would ever find it. I never showed it to anyone.

I hadn't thought about that incident since I was nine years old. Toward the end of art class, we went around in a circle sharing our art-making process. When it came my turn, I talked about that art fair and the big, black, ugly mistake I had made. Judy, who was sitting under her watercolor landscape that resembled Monet's *Lily Pond*, confessed, "I never used to like anything I created. Gradually, I started using art as a way to express my emotions and my emotions as a way to express my art. In time, I came to see the beauty in what I created, no matter how wonderful or difficult the emotion."

From that point on, I worked diligently expressing my emotions like my anger, hurt, and sadness through art. I knew an artist existed in me somewhere, and I wanted more than anything to find her.

# Falling

After I met Steve, I began attending Agape service every Sunday morning with him. I'd never been much into church in my youth. Even though I had attended parochial schools most of my life, my parents weren't all that interested in religious life. When it came to religion, there were no pretenses; their priority was to give us "the best possible education," and for them that meant attending Catholic schools. They weren't churchgoers either; they were big drinkers and social creatures. They loved going to parties and entertaining family and friends at home with elaborate dinner gatherings. At least one weekend a month, Mom would spend an entire Saturday cleaning the house and cooking a roast beef for six to eight friends that evening. They'd stay up really late, drinking, smoking, and laughing, with Tony Bennett, Vic Damone, and Brenda Lee blasting on the stereo. Since most of their social events took place on Saturday evenings, Sunday mornings were usually reserved for recuperation time.

Sunday was not church going time for them, but it was for us kids. Every Sunday morning like clockwork, Dad drove my two brothers and I to church. He'd drop us off at 8:45 by the post office flagpole near the curbside, next to the horseshoe driveway in front of the church. Then an hour and a half later, he'd pick us up at that same location. It didn't take long for my brothers and I to discover we didn't *really* have to attend church service. By the time I was eleven, we figured out that all we had to do was make an appearance of going to church. Once Dad dropped us off, we'd walk around the half circle driveway, along the concrete and black wrought-iron fence walkway, up the shiny stone steps, and through the main wooden double doors. Together we walked down the red-carpeted center aisle, and one by one, we bowed our heads, kneeling as we made the sign of the cross in front of the altar. Then in single file formation, out the side door we went.

We'd spend the next eighty minutes hanging out at Dunkin' Donuts across the street, using the money we were supposed to give as an offering to buy donuts and juice. Just when mass was about to end, we'd walk back to church, sneak in the rear entrance, and grab the weekly bulletin that gave an outline of the sermon and list of activities for the upcoming week, proof to Mom of our attendance. I spent most of my life believing our weekly church attendance was based on my parent's desire to have peace and quiet on Sunday mornings, rather than for any pious reasons. I never had any of that Catholic guilt over our ritual to ditch church. As an adult, I actually chuckled at our ingenuity.

Though on those rare occasions when we did attend church as a family for a special event like a baptism or wedding, I eased into the service, surrendering to the majestic holy surroundings. I even found great amusement from heartwarming stories of redemption and remarkable accounts of performed miracles. But looking back, I was grateful I only had to attend service every once in a while.

I hadn't set foot in a church, other than for a special event, since I was a girl. Timmy and Tessy hadn't been raised as churchgoers. I never thought to ask my sister about her beliefs, probably because I assumed she, like me, didn't have much faith in the whole thing. But when I began attending service at Agape, something shifted. A radiant spirit filled the room. I felt peaceful, touched by a kind of uplifting from the angelic voices of the choir. I felt the first rays of sun upon me, like a flower opening under holy skies. And I felt sanctified looking around at all the luminous faces surrounding me.

Now that I was a parent, I thought it was important and my responsibility to introduce some form of spiritual life to the kids. I wanted something more for them than what I had received. I wanted them to have a sense of something bigger than themselves. I wanted them to know there existed places where people went to worship the spirit or life force that exists in all beings. I found an organization in Santa Cruz that was practicing the teachings taught at Agape. The minister's name was Sandy. She was a lovely, wholesome woman, a schoolteacher type in her mid-fifties, who had the ladylike manners of June Cleaver.

"But church is boring," Timmy protested, when I told him my plan for how we were going to spend our Sunday mornings.

"Have you ever been to church?" I asked.

With a grimace face, he replied, "No. But it's boring."

"They have an arts and crafts class for kids in the back room during service. You can attend church service every other week and on the alternating weeks, you can attend the craft class. Does that work?" I asked.

"But crafts are for *girls*," he whined.

"Well, we're going to church as a family every week. And it's your choice if you want to attend church or craft class," I finally told him.

After our first church experience, I took the kids to Toys R Us and bought them each a bicycle. It wasn't a bribe. Once school started, it didn't take the kids long to notice other kids riding their bikes to and from school.

"Auntie, can we get bicycles? I want to ride my bike to school, just like the other kids," Timmy asked, while driving home from school one day.

"Yeah, sure, we can go buy a couple of bikes. That sounds okay. But I don't think you'll be riding your bike to school."

"Why? All the other kids do," he shrugged.

"Well, I'm sure they live a lot closer than we do. We live four miles from school. And two of those miles are up a steep mountain."

"I can do it. I can bike the mountain, no problem."

Though it wasn't realistic for Timmy to ride his bike to and from school, he sounded convincing. He always said things in a way that made me think twice. It took me a while to figure out Timmy was a boy with big ideas, who at times was overconfident, even cocky. I tried to say *yes* to the kids as much as possible. Not because of the pity I felt for them, but because I wanted them to live in a world full of possibilities. I wanted them to have a sense they could do and be anything they wanted.

We had a blast picking out bicycles that Sunday. There must've been a dozen bikes for each of them to choose from, and they looked at all their options very carefully.

"This is the one I want, Auntie," said Timmy, with his two hands holding onto the handlebars of a red metallic six-speed twenty-inch Raleigh mountain bike.

"Are you sure?" I asked.

"Yep, I'm sure. This is just like my friend Ryan's bike," he replied, radiating a smile as he flipped through the gears.

I turned to Tessy and asked, "Have you made your decision, Princess?"

"I think I like this one the best," she said, sitting on the flowered banana seat of a sixteen-inch pink speckled Huffy bike. It had iridescent tassels hanging from the handlebars.

"I've always wanted a bike with tassels," she said, swaying her fingers through the dangling fringe. "And look Auntie, the pink flowers on my sundress match the flowers on the basket and seat."

I borrowed the house van so we could transport the assembled bikes home that day. As we drove back to the house, the early afternoon sunlight spilled into the van as the kids beamed smiles brighter than I'd ever seen before. They talked continuously about all the people they were going to show their new bikes to. Once we arrived home, I stood at the top of the hill and watched them cycle the long paved driveway a couple of times. Timmy took the lead, giving Tessy instructions on how to properly ride the new terrain.

"Tessy, make sure you stay on the right side of the driveway, just like this. We're supposed to ride on the *right* side of the road, just like cars and trucks do. Oh yeah, when you're about to ride down the hill, slow down and bring your foot and pedal back, almost into braking position, like this." She watched carefully as he rode around the parked cars a few times before taking off down the steep driveway.

After I watched and waited for them to go around a few more times, I said to them, "You kids all set now? I'm going back to my room. Have fun and be careful. If you need me, you know where to find me. Okay?"

"Yep," yelled Timmy, cycling up the hill.

"Okay," said Tessy, who was parked on the side of the driveway re-arranging her blue backpack in the flower basket.

I walked back to my room, curled up on the white wicker rocking chair sitting in the now mid-day sun, and began reading a book.

Fifteen minutes later, Timmy came running up to the open eight-foot sliding glass door, panting, almost out of breath. Panicking, he yelled, "Auntie! Tessy's been hurt! Tessy fell off her bike and she's *really* hurt!"

"What?" I swallowed hard as I jumped up out of the chair, dropping my book on the floor.

I headed toward Timmy, who was now standing on the entrance rug in the doorway. He leaned over, placed his hands on top of his knees, trying to catch his breath.

"Where is she?" I gasped, as my heart began to pound fast. Somewhere in the distance I could hear faint cries, like the yelp of a wounded animal. I called out to her frantically, "Tessy, where are you?" Then I stood quietly, trying to listen to the direction of her cries.

Seconds later, she limped into sight from around the corner of the house. Her face was red as she cried hysterically. Her right hand was in a fist wiping her red swollen eyes. Her left arm was drooping. She couldn't speak; she was almost hyperventilating as she found her way into my arms.

"My Princess. Oh, my baby. I'm here. I'm right here," I said nervously, as I picked her up and threw a white cashmere blanket around her. I sat down in the rocking chair with her on top of me. She pulled her knees up into her chest and buried her bawling face into my chest. I quickly scanned her body, checking for blood and to see if any parts of her body were disjointed. The only injury I found was a badly skinned and bloodied knee.

"She was riding her bike down the hill near Susan's house. She was going too fast. She yelled for me to help her. I told her to put on her brakes. But she lost control and hit the tree near the tree house, she fell," explained Timmy.

Her entire body shook and sobbed as she quivered in my arms. I closed my eyes, rocking her back and forth, holding her closely as I took long, deep breaths, hoping it would ease her.

"I'll go tell Wendy and Michael. Maybe Susan can help. She's a nurse. I'll be right back, Auntie," said Timmy. He was gone before I could respond.

Within a couple of minutes, Tessy's sobbing stopped and her body lay lifeless in my arms. For a second, I thought she had stopped breathing. I panicked. My pulse raced as I pulled back the blanket. I breathed a heavy sigh of relief realizing the accident had been so traumatizing for her, that she had cried herself to sleep.

It poured all morning long the following day. After I dropped the kids off at school, I immediately drove back home, and headed straight for the kids' room. I needed to be surrounded by the things Tessy loved most. Moving slower than normal, I straightened up their room, picking clothes up off the floor and placing them into the wicker hamper. I stacked Timmy's Super Nintendo games, organized Tessy's Barbie display, and placed the pink pig Tessy made in ceramic class, back on top of her nightstand. I flipped through Tessy's new princess glitter sticker book and then made Timmy's bed. He had insisted on taking the top bunk, which was fine with Tessy because she was afraid of heights.

As I crouched down low to make Tessy's bed, I felt cracked and fragile as tears of heartache gushed down my face. I was flooded with guilt and blamed myself for her accident, for not being there for her, for not watching and protecting her properly. With my hand gripping my aching stomach, I crawled into Tessy's bed as the sound of rain pounded against the windows, and cried myself to sleep.

# An Unresolved Past

Joan taught me the value of giving the kids choices. "When parents play the puppeteer, pulling the strings for their kids rather than allowing them to have *some* control, it can lead to unhealthy power struggles between a parent and their child," she once told me. During my visits back East, I'd watch her give her kids choices all the time. They were simple selections, like, "What do you want for lunch? You can have either a hamburger or grilled cheese sandwich." Lots of times Timmy and Tessy wanted different things; he wanted a thick juicy burger, and she wanted a hot dog. That never bothered Joan. She'd cook each of them whatever they wanted. What was more important for Joan was for the kids to have a sense of control while building their independence and identity.

I'd never had much of an attachment to the word "aunt." As a young girl, I preferred calling my aunts by their first name. It made me feel grown up. But Mom thought otherwise. "It's impolite," she'd say. "Calling your relatives *aunt* is a way of showing them respect." But I never saw it that way. More than anything I wanted to feel grown up.

So early on I gave the kids a choice on what they could call me. Isn't that what we do? Don't we raise our children the way we wished we had been raised? They decided to call me "Auntie." I was quite pleased with their decision.

When we moved to Santa Cruz, everyone started calling me "Auntie." Anytime I was introduced to someone, I was always presented as "Auntie." I don't think half the people I met ever knew my birth name. It was very sweet, endearing actually. It made me feel special. I'd never had a nickname before. Well, actually I had. And I hated it! As a kid, my family used to call me "Big Mouth." Can you imagine going through childhood being called *Big Mouth*? I guess I had strong opinions I wasn't afraid to speak, even as a child.

Once the kids and I settled in Santa Cruz, Dad dutifully sent us a check every month. I didn't want to accept it. I prided myself on being self-sufficient. Since the age of seventeen, I had never asked, nor had I ever taken money from either of my parents. Not even when Dad offered to pay my student loan off many years ago. What I came to eventually realize was that all those years in the business world was in some way my needing to prove something to myself. I'd become a strong, capable, independent woman. I strived for perfection and possessed a professional demeanor in everything I did. It seemed like an easy, if not natural role for me. But while taking care of the kids, I discovered I also had needs and vulnerabilities. My biggest challenge was reaching out, asking for help and support, something I had little experience with.

The one thing you can count on in life is that it's always changing. Since I didn't have enough money saved to take care of the kids for the entire year, I accepted Dad's support. I felt awkward taking his money, feeling as if I were some kind of loser not being able to sufficiently provide for the kids and myself. I was truly grateful to Wendy and Michael for extending their home and hearts to us. I felt the presence of grace growing in our lives; mostly by the way we were being supported by the generosity of others.

Susan, Briana's mom, offered great assistance to me early on. She was a mother who knew only too well the challenges of motherhood. At first I didn't understand the comradery that oftentimes develops between mothers—like when she offered to watch Timmy and Tessy on Tuesday nights for three hours so I could attend a local parenting therapy group.

While cleaning up after dinner one evening and discussing the details of the class and our schedules, I said to her, "Thanks so much for helping me out. I'd be happy to do something for you in return."

"That's not necessary, Auntie. I'm happy to help you out," was her reply.

I'd always reciprocated an act of kindness. In my narrow thinking, I couldn't fully comprehend that I didn't need to give something back in return. But it was Susan who taught me, without words, what so many mothers around the world do. They pick each other up, listen, encourage, and support one another, even if it means stepping into another's shoes when you're weary and battered to the bone.

Even though I had the help and support of many, I found myself, more than once, fantasizing about another life—one filled with travel, tropics, and long moonlit nights strolling along a balmy beach with a lover. Sometimes I wanted to be anywhere but where I was. I felt alive, and I was learning and growing from my experience with the kids. Plus I was developing a great fondness for my new extended family. But at the same time, I felt like I was disappearing. I didn't know who I was anymore. My entire existence revolved around the kids, or at least it felt that way.

Being with Tessy's fears and insecurities was oftentimes difficult for me. I was barraged with memories of my own childhood. Painful ones. Like the time when I was her age and *my* mother went into the hospital. I not only lost my mom for a period of time, but my dad was missing in action. I didn't see him for almost the entire time my mother was in the hospital. I felt so alone and abandoned, unsure if I was ever going to see my family again. I felt torn up on the inside, helpless in my ability to be there for Tessy at times because old, painful feelings of being deserted were so real in present day time. For the first time, I can honestly say, I was beginning to get a glimpse of the wounded, aching child I had carried inside myself and my unresolved past.

## Staying Home

Early one Saturday morning after breakfast, I walked into the kid's room and said, "Okay guys, it's time to get ready. We've got lots of errands to run." Then I quickly scanned the room to see what chores needed to be done before we left.

"Oh, dang it. Do we *have* to go?" asked Timmy. He was sitting on the floor playing with his Super Nintendo. "I don't wanna go anywhere. Can't we just stay home today in our pajamas?"

"Yeah, Auntie. Can't we stay home in our pajamas, just this once?" asked Tessy, who was sitting at the play-table putting stickers into her new Rainbow Fish sticker book.

I stopped for a moment and thought to myself, *I remember staying home in my pajamas all day.* Then I peered out the window at the dense gray sky and the blustering autumn wind. A light drizzle had just started.

I shrugged my shoulders, in a good way, turned toward the kids and said, "Okay, we can stay home in our pajamas today."

"Hooray! Yippee! We get to stay home! We can stay in our pajamas!" they cheered.

Tessy lifted the edge of her Minnie Mouse nightgown, twirling round and round like a ballerina. Timmy came up to me and with the force of a linebacker, wrapped both arms around my waist, giving me a great big squeeze, while saying, "Thank you Auntie. You're the best."

I liked hearing the kids say, "You're the best" or "You're awesome." Of course, they mostly said those words when I gave them what they wanted, when they heard that little three-letter word "yes". We didn't really do anything that day; we just hung out in our pajamas. That's all. But it was a very good day for all of us.

A few mornings later, I woke to a faint knock on my bedroom door. While peeking her head into my room, Tessy moaned, "Auntie, I don't feel good."

I pulled back the comforter, rolled my body back a few inches, and patted the warm spot I'd just been lying in. She slid in, like a hand gracefully slipping into a glove, and then I spooned her while snuggling the comforter up under her chin.

"What's the matter, Princess?" I moved my right hand onto her forehead. She didn't have a fever.

"I don't feel good, Auntie," she meekly repeated.

"What doesn't feel good, baby?"

"I have a tummy ache."

"Ohhh," I said, and gently kissed the back of her head as I snuggled her closer.

"Can I stay home from school today?" she asked.

*Was she really sick? Or did she just want to stay home with me?* I wasn't sure how to tell. My mind instantly reflected back to the previous night—what she had eaten, what she had done, what state she had been in when she went to bed. I had played Barbies with her after dinner—it was a rare event. Tessy had been asking me for some time to play Barbies or help her with her sticker books. Most of the time I told her I was too busy. But on that particular night, I was tired of all the excuses I'd been giving her—and myself.

So after dinner, we sprawled out on the living room floor in front of a crackling fire. Michael, who was sitting on the teal green chair with his elbows resting on his knees, and Timmy, who was sitting crossed-legged on the floor, were strategizing over countless games of checkers. Tessy, Briana, and I laid on our stomachs with half a dozen coloring books on the floor and a carousel of Crayola Crayons. After we colored for a while, Tessy stood up and said, "Just stay there, Auntie. Don't go anywhere, *please*," and then skipped out of the room. Moments later she reappeared carrying in both her hands Briana's vintage round orange suitcase full of Barbie dolls, clothes, and accessories. The three of us sat cross-legged dressing Barbie and her friends for almost an hour. Not only did Tessy go to bed very happy that night, she didn't come knocking on my door scared and lonely later in the evening.

"Sure, Princess, you can stay home," I told her, just before I remembered I had a therapy appointment at noon.

I didn't want to miss out on my session with Tony. Even though we'd only seen him a few times, I was getting some much needed guidance from him. I saw him only every other week. On the alternating weeks, the kids and I saw him as a family. If I canceled my appointment, it'd be a whole two weeks before I'd see him alone again. I couldn't wait; I had things I *needed* to talk to him about.

The prior week while in family session, I had vented to Tony how, "Timmy never picks up his stuff. I give him fifteen, twenty minutes to clean his room, and when I go back twenty minutes, even half an hour later, ninety percent of the time his room is still a mess. His stuff is all over the floor: his checkers, clothes, books, homework and Nintendo games. He even leaves his backpack in the *middle* of the room. I don't get it. Why can't he put his school bag on the chair? And he never puts his dirty clothes *in* the laundry basket. His clothes end up around the basket or halfway in the basket, but never fully *in* the basket. And every time I walk into the bathroom, there are towels all over the floor. Can't they just put the towels on one of the *three* towel racks?" I knew I was harping, but I was frustrated. The kids just didn't get it. And I didn't get why they didn't get it, or why they couldn't or wouldn't listen to me.

Tony suggested I focus on what they do correctly, rather than what they don't do.

"It's like this," he said, as he placed his pen and pad on the table. "Try to restrain from the urge to be critical. Making the kids feel good about themselves will reinforce good behavior. So instead of complaining about the clothes that don't make it into the basket, focus on the clothes that *do* make it in."

Okay, I was willing to try it, so I did as he suggested. First, I stopped yelling and complaining. Then a couple of days after our session, I walked into the bathroom and saw a towel on the floor and another on the chrome towel rack. When I entered their bedroom, I said, "Good job, guys. Whoever put the towel on the towel rack, way to go," and left it at that. The next time I went into their bathroom, both towels were on the racks. In less than one week's time, I was surprised to see how things had changed. Nothing big, but it was a start. I *needed* to keep my appointment with Tony. He was helping me to stay sane in the unpredictable world of being a new parent.

Tessy stayed cozy in my bed as I helped Timmy get ready for school. Meanwhile, I checked in with Wendy and Michael to find out what their schedules were for the day, knowing they were leaving on a trip the following morning. They both had plans to leave the house by late morning.

"Maggie will be here all day," said Wendy, sipping a cup of coffee in her office. Maggie was Wendy's secretary. She had two kids of her own, teenagers. She liked Timmy and Tessy and was very kind to them.

After I dropped Timmy off at school, I came home, and while folding a basket of laundry in the kid's room to keep Tessy company, I told her, "I have an appointment with Tony today, Princess. So I'll be leaving at 11:30. I'll be home by 1:30. Okay?"

Looking up from her Dr. Seuss book, she asked, "But," she hesitated, "who'll take care of me while you're gone?"

"Maggie's here today, all day," I replied.

"But, I want *you* to take care of me," she said, with her index finger pulling on her lower lip.

"I will take care of your for most of the day, Princess. It's only for two hours. Okay?" I said and smiled.

The only TV in the house was upstairs, in the family-media room. I didn't let the kids watch TV that much; instead, they watched movies. I made a little bed for Tessy on the sofa in the family room, with her Pocahontas pillow and blue and white afghan her mother had crocheted for her years ago. Tessy toted her Barbies and coloring books with her. I placed a plastic cup of orange juice on the coffee table, put on a Cinderella video before I kissed her goodbye, and left. It was the first time she had been in the house without me.

When I arrived home a few minutes before 1:30, I entered the house and yelled, "Tessy, I'm home."

There was no response.

I walked into the family room. She wasn't there. I called her name out a few times as I picked up my pace, looking in the kitchen, living room, then Wendy's office, before I finally reached her bedroom. There I found her weeping in her bed.

"What's the matter, Princess? Why are you crying?" I asked, as I bent down and sat on her bed.

In her softest voice, she said, "I was so scared. You weren't here. I didn't know what to do after the movie ended. I came down to my room and cried. I missed you so much, Auntie," she said, rubbing her eyes. Then she hugged me tighter than I had ever been hugged before.

I kissed my index finger and gently pressed it against her lips. I snuggled into bed with her, cupping myself around her body, holding her thin wrists in my hands. I felt the bittersweet of motherhood. I felt the weight of her dependency; it was heavy at times. Yet the charm of her need and love for me warmed and filled the silent parts of myself.

Later that afternoon, when Timmy came home from school, he walked straight into his bedroom, changed into his bathing suit, and took off to go play in the hot tub with Briana.

Seeing Timmy in action, Tessy, who was playing with her Barbies in her bed, asked in a chirpy voice, "Auntie, can I go in the hot tub too?"

"But you're sick," I said, gazing at her over the top of my eyeglasses.

"I feel better now," she said, smiling.

"Well, Tessy, the way it works is, if anyone stays home from school because they're sick, they need to spend the *entire* day in bed so they can get the rest they need to get well again. So that means no swimming and no playing with Timmy or Briana. You need to stay in your bed and get well. Maybe later on tonight after dinner we'll watch a movie together."

Her smile vanished. She didn't like what I said. But I ended up stopping that issue from ever popping up again, because for the remaining school year, she never asked to stay home again.

# A Bad Dream

I awoke from the most horrifying nightmare I'd ever had in my entire life! You know—the kind that shakes and rattles you at your core. It made me want to jump out of my own skin. In my dream, Timmy, Tessy and I were in a large empty house. A faceless man dressed in a long, black trench coat was chasing after us, trying to kill us. He grabbed hold of Tessy by her hair and with a straight razor, tortured her by cutting three-inch incisions all over her body. She was screaming in anguish, with her arms extended toward me, pleading and crying for me to help her. I was terrorized, unable to go to her rescue because I'd been belted and strapped down to the top of a black leather-examining table.

My little one was experiencing the worst thing I could ever have imagined, and I was absolutely helpless. I was breathing hard and heavy, gasping for air. When I woke up, I was breathing the same hard and heavy breath I had been experiencing in my dream. I knew it was only a dream, but it was so intense, it felt so real.

Feeling flushed and disoriented, I sat upright in my bed, turned on the Tiffany table lamp, and began taking long slow deep breaths trying to bring my breathing back to normal. I pushed the comforter off my sweaty body, reached over, grabbed the phone, and dialed my dad. I looked over at the clock. It was 1:33 a.m., which meant it was 4:33 in the morning his time. Realizing the time, I almost hung up, knowing my call would most likely wake him. But I couldn't. I needed to talk to someone.

"Hello," he muttered in a groggy voice.

"Hi, Dad. It's me. I'm sorry to call you so late at night," there was a crack in my voice. I was fighting tears.

"It's okay, dear. What's the matter?" he asked calmly.

After a few seconds of silence, with my body still shaking and feeling the strain of trying to contain and hold myself together, I finally burst into tears. Sobbing, I narrated to him, in between gasps of breath, my horrible nightmare.

After a long pause and an enormous exhale, I said, "I *love* them *so* much, Dad. I want Joan to get better. But what if she *does*? What then? I'm gonna have to give them back. I'm not sure I want to." There was anguish in my voice. I shocked myself hearing me speak those words for the first time. For a moment, I could no longer remember who I had been before they won my heart.

A few mornings later, I arrived home after dropping the kids off at school. The telephone was ringing as I walked into my bedroom. I hurried, almost tripping over the carpet, trying to answer it. Dad was on the other end.

"I just spoke with your sister's therapist. You know she's been in the program for over five months now. He told me Joan might not ever be well enough to take care of her children." His tone was serious, even dire.

"Why?"

"They're not seeing the progress they'd hoped for by this time."

"Have you talked to Joan about it?" I asked, cradling the phone on my shoulder while cracking the window open above my desk.

"No. And I'm not going to. You know a lot can happen from now until the time she completes the program."

Staring out the window at the rainy wetness on the enormous redwood tree, I said, "Yeah, that makes sense."

"I just thought I'd let you know," he said, in a way that made me sense he was discouraged.

After I hung up, an inner silent torment emerged. On the one hand, I had to admit, there was a part of me that shouted with exuberant joy, *yes, they're mine!* On the other hand, I heard a begrudging voice saying, *like forever? What about my life?*

Right around that time I started writing morning pages again. I had read Julia Cameron's *The Artist's Way* a few years back and was faithful in writing three morning pages every day. She offers it as a tool to help get those bits and pieces that run wild in your head, out of your head. It was helping me let go some of my pent-up frustrations, instead of carrying them around all day. Every morning, as soon as I woke up, I pulled out my yellow legal notepad, and jotted down whatever came to mind: a dream, lists of the things I needed to do for the day ahead of me, my complaints, aspirations, even my fears. I wrote it all down, every morning. I felt a cleansing from it. It was like a mini therapy session with myself.

Some of the things I'd been writing about lately were the disappointing feelings that had begun to surface around my childhood and my dad. I couldn't say I had had a special relationship with him in my youth. Actually, he had scared the hell out of me; he was a big, stocky guy who was always barking commands and seemed generally angry, or at minimum not happy most of the time, unless of course he was drinking. He had been a vague presence in my life as a child, a ghost—or maybe I was the ghost, because he never showed much of an interest in me.

He was half-hearted in his love for his family. His passion came in the form of numbers, dogs, and cards; he loved to gamble. He was a schoolteacher and took a second job as a taxi cab driver at night to help make ends meet. But he wasn't just driving cab at night. After he completed his rounds, he'd spend the remainder of the evening attending private poker games in the back of smoke-filled bar rooms. On the days he didn't drive a cab, he spent the latter part of the afternoon catching the last few races at the Raynham dog track.

Mostly what I remembered was that whenever we gathered for celebrations, he was the one organizing cribbage or poker games for small change. He put a brand new deck of blue Bicycle playing cards in his glove box every so often. Anytime we visited friends or relatives, he'd lean over from the driver's seat, open the glove box, pull out a deck of cards, and place it in his shirt pocket. He was always ready for an opportunity.

Our relationship changed when I was sixteen. By that time I'd run away from home a few times. It wasn't as bad as it sounds. Basically my strategy was, whenever I was grounded and not allowed to go out with my friends, I'd pack a bag before I left for school on Friday morning, and then slip in the back door late Sunday night. I usually slept at a friend's house, without her parent's knowledge, just in case mom tried to track me down. The last time I had run away, Mom actually called the police. "It's the legal thing, I *had* to," she later said in her defense.

When I returned home, I had to show up for a court appearance. I sat for hours in the lobby of the juvenile courthouse waiting for my name to be called. Dad took the day off from school; he was the more rational one when it came to *those kinds of matters*. Outside the courtroom, Dad and I sat opposite from each other, on separate dark wooden benches that looked like church pews. He sat serenely reading the newspaper while I stared at the large black and white wall clock. We didn't say a word to one another. The silence wasn't difficult; it was normal. When my name was finally called, both Dad and I stood before the bald-headed judge as he rustled through papers.

He took off his wire-rimmed glasses, cleared his throat, then addressed my dad, "Mr. Maher, the records indicate your daughter Laura has run away a number of times. Is that correct?"

"Yes, Your Honor, that's correct," responded Dad, with his hands clasped together in front of his blue plaid polyester suit coat.

"And there's been drug involvement." It wasn't really a question.

"Yes, Your Honor. To what extent we don't know," was Dad's honest reply. His face was blank, maybe drained, maybe sad or maybe worn by it all. I couldn't tell.

I waited in silence, not caring much about my fate. The judge ordered me to enter into a local drug treatment facility called the Phaneuf Center for two weeks, beginning that afternoon. Neither Dad nor I were expecting things to go that way. But going there didn't really bother me. I was happy to get away for a bit of time since I was still fuming at Mom for calling the cops.

Much to my surprise, by the time I returned home two weeks later, Dad was in AA and had stopped drinking. Years later he told me, "It was that day in the courtroom when I realized there was something wrong. I knew it wasn't your fault, being sent to a drug rehab. I knew the problem started with me. Later that night, while sitting at the bar drinking a cold beer after retiring my cab, I knew it was my last drink."

When I arrived home after my stay at the drug treatment center, he was suddenly interested in me, as his daughter, as a person. He had changed and became a better man, and I grew to love and respect him for it.

But while caring for Timmy and Tessy, old painful childhood memories began to plague me. I spent weeks, with Tony's suggestion and encouragement, making lists of all my disappointments. Tony also instructed me to write letters from the wounded little girl in me to my dad, telling him how hurt I had felt as a child. "You don't need to send the letters," Tony advised. "It's just a tool to help you get in touch with your feelings."

One night, after I put the kids to bed, I finally mustered up enough nerve to call my dad and talk to him about some of those things I'd been writing about. He was surprised by my call, but willing to hear me out. While sitting at my desk, tightly gripping the phone in one hand and the receiver in the other, I told him how abandoned I felt by him as a child.

After I said everything I needed to say, I finally asked him, "When Mom went into the hospital when I was a little girl, I didn't want to go live with relatives. I wanted you to take care of me. Where were you Dad? Why didn't you take care of us?"

He replied with, "You know, your mother was a difficult woman to be around."

I cut him off before he could say anything else, "Dad, this isn't about Mom. It's about *you* and *me*."

There was a long, silent pause.

After a heavy sigh, his voice softened and he said, "You're right." Then he breathed slow and long a few times, before he added, "You know, Laura, I'll never get the Father of the Year award. I live with that every day since my sobriety. I'm sorry I wasn't there for you and your brothers and sister. I've made a lot of mistakes. All I can say is, I'm truly sorry."

Living a human life is anything but perfect. When we acknowledge, accept, and embrace those parts of ourselves we push away and deny, light shines on the dark, and we transform our demons into something more positive.

What changed for my dad and I was that we came to intimately understand one another, even in our blunders—or maybe because of them. What made a long lasting impression on me was when Dad took responsibility for his absence. After he got sober and started working on becoming a better person, he inspired me to be the best I could be. His remorse and accountability for the ways he hadn't been available to his family, made me want to take responsibility for my own actions, for all the ways I hadn't looked deep inside myself. By forgiving him, I was learning how to clean up my messy, wounded life.

## Holiday Times

One weekend a month, the kids and I traveled down to Los Angles. It was a way to give Wendy and Michael a break so they could have their house to themselves since the kids and I took up quite a bit of space. But mostly we did it because I missed being with my friends. Timmy and Tessy loved to travel. I'd pick them up late Friday morning from school with the back seat packed with blankets, pillows, food, and games. We listened to books on tape and music (Timmy was fond of Seal's "Kiss From a Rose", and Tessy loved TLC's "Waterfalls"). We also played spelling bees, math games, and I Spy too. And of course, no road trip was complete without seeing who could spot the most out-of-state license plates.

Days before we left to spend the Christmas holiday in L.A., I spilled the beans. I didn't mean to, but I did, and I felt as though I tarnished Tessy's innocence forever. Susan had offered to pick Tessy up from school. It was planned ahead of time for Timmy to spend the afternoon at his friend Brandon's house.

I was in the laundry room folding clothes when Tessy announced, "Auntie, I'm home."

"I'm in the laundry room, Princess. I'll be right there," I yelled back, then grabbed the handles of the creaky wicker basket and headed back to my bedroom.

Tessy stood at the sliding glass door of the entryway to my room with her blonde bangs slightly covering her eyes. She was balancing, rather successfully, her blue backpack over her right shoulder and an orange writing journal between her elbow and rib cage. In her two hands she carried her coat, an uneaten apple, and her purse.

"Need some help there?" I asked, as I entered the room.

"Yes, Auntie. I can't take off my shoes to come into the room." She was loyal to the "no shoes in the house" agreement.

I carefully took hold of her items and placed them on top of the desk. She slid the backpack off, and I swooped in, grabbing her under her armpits, half twirling her into my lap as we sat down in the white rocking chair together. It was effortless taking hold of her; she was light as a feather.

"Let's take off your shoes while you tell me about your day," I said, as I leaned over her and pulled her black patent leather shoes off her feet.

Suddenly, she jumped out of my lap, making a faint thump on the wooden floor, and stood in front of me with eyes wide.

"Auntie," she said, "I'm a big girl now. I know there's no Santa Claus. I know it's just what parents tell their kids, and the presents *really* come from our mom and dad." She stood tall and proud, lifting her chin up in the air with her hands clasped behind her back.

"How, who, who told you that?" I patted my thighs a couple of times, motioning her to come back into my lap, but she refused my invitation with a shake of her head.

"Kids from school." She nodded, then smiled, looking quite satisfied with herself.

I was sad, disappointed actually. I saw this event to be a pivotal moment in losing a bit of childhood, never again to be touched. To me, childhood was about believing in a mythical world of make believe and magic. Weren't fairy tales and fantasies an expected part of the innocence of children, a needed requirement in developing and expanding one's imagination? Why, she was only seven years old! I wanted Tessy to stay pure and live in the world of child-like faith and wonderment. My heart was crushed.

"Oh, Princess, how do you feel about that?" I asked, reaching for her hand.

"It's okay, Auntie, I'm a big girl now," she repeated, swaying from side to side.

I reached for her hand and looked down, studying her pink chipped fingernail polish.

I finally looked up at her face and said, "I'm so disappointed for you. I feel sad that you're only seven years old and learning there's no Santa Claus or tooth fairy."

Immediately her body stiffened, like a tin soldier. Her eyes got bigger, wider, as her mouth dropped open. She yanked her hand out of mine, took a step back, and said, "What? What do you mean? There's no tooth fairy?"

I could've just crumpled up and died.

The day before Christmas, Shirley hosted a small holiday celebration at her home in Los Angeles. She greeted us at her front door when we arrived. Once Tessy was in the house, she handed Shirley the plate of homemade chocolate chip cookies she carried in from the car and said, "Here, Shirley, these are for you. We baked them ourselves. But Auntie used salt instead of sugar. They taste, ah, okay I guess."

I rolled my eyes at Shirley and said, "Can't keep anything a secret around them." We smiled and then laughed.

Not too long after we settled in, the kids wanted to open the presents Shirley had for them under the tree.

"Can I go first?" asked Timmy excitedly. He was standing next to me holding his gift with both hands. "Tessy *always* goes first because she's a *girl*."

"Sure, you can go first," I said, tapping the cushion on the couch, inviting him to sit next to me.

He was thrilled to get a yellow plastic Wiffle ball and bat.

Next was Britney's turn. She was Alicia's daughter, one of Shirley's closest friends. Britney was a dark-haired five year-old who was awfully shy and mostly stayed close to her mother. Alicia was sitting on the white leather chair next to the couch. Britney propped herself in between her mother's knees and opened a beautiful dark-haired Barbie doll wearing a long red sequenced evening dress.

Finally it was Tessy's turn. She sat across from me on the floor, cross-legged, and with great enthusiasm tore open her gift.

"Old Maid cards?" she said. Her upper lip rose to a sneer.

I got nervous witnessing her response, wondering what she'd do next.

I tried to act fast by saying, "Awesome. I love Old Maid. Can we play a game, *right now*?"

"No! I don't want Old Maid cards!" she snapped back. Turning her head, she glared over at Britney, who was hugging her new Barbie.

"Well, I use to have Old Maid cards when I was a girl, and I loved them," I said, sitting on the edge of the couch trying to smile.

"Well I don't!" said Tessy, as she picked the cards up from her lap and threw them across the room.

One of Tessy's behavior issues, which I had noticed early on, was that every once in a while she got intensely jealous and visibly upset when she was in direct contact with a young girl who was with her mother, especially a doting mother. It was easy for me to tell when she'd get into one of those tough places; she'd purse her lips, draw her brows together, and would give the young girl a cross-eyed look. Sometimes she'd say mean things like, "I don't like you," or "I don't want to play with you," while staring the little girl down. Just a month earlier, Tessy had been coloring with a young friend of Briana's. Her mommy walked into Briana's bedroom and commented to her daughter what a lovely picture she was coloring. I witnessed Tessy break and throw crayons at the little girl in a fit of rage. I even once saw her push a small girl who was visiting Lori in Hawaii. I was on edge and never knew quite what to expect. I just learned to manage my way through it all by observing her and jumping in if Tessy was about to do something I felt could be dangerous.

The odd thing was, about a week or so after she received those Old Maid cards from Shirley, I watched Tessy place them in her blue quilted backpack, the one her mom had given her, the one she placed all her prized possessions in, and carry them around everywhere she went for the remaining school year.

On New Year's Eve day, we left L.A. for the six-hour drive back to Santa Cruz. I don't know how it came up in conversation, but we started talking about the meaning of New Year's.

"New Year's is a time when we acknowledge all the events that have occurred during the past year. We say goodbye to the old year and welcome in the coming year with our desires and goals," I said, occasionally glancing at the kids in the rear view mirror.

"Can you name some of the events that have taken place during this past year?"

"We left our home in Brockton and moved to California,"

Timmy shouted.

"Mom had her stroke," answered Tessy.

"Yep," I said, nodding my head.

"And we have a new sister, Briana," Timmy offered.

With her elbow on her knee, tapping her forehead, Tessy said, "We went to Hawaii. And every month we go to Los Angeles."

"Yeah, that's right, Princess," I said, encouragingly.

"I'm going to Tae Kwon Do every week," said Timmy, beaming a smile.

"And I'm in dance class, Auntie, and choir practice too. I've always wanted to be in choir practice."

"Yep."

"We're in a new school and I have a new best friend, Brandon," said Timmy, striking the console with his hand.

"That's right. Great job guys! Now, what about your goals for the New Year? What do you *want* for this coming year?" I asked.

After a brief silence, Tessy replied, in a soft, melancholy voice, "I wanna be back home with my mommy."

With damp eyes, Timmy added, "Yeah, me too," as he stared out the window into the early night sky, as a light rain began to fall.

# *Bonds*

One stormy Friday evening, we all gathered in the family room to watch a movie. Wendy, Michael, Susan, and I sat on the sofa. Tessy and Briana snuggled under a blue fleece blanket on the sofa chair with Shanti, Wendy's Pomeranian, nuzzled in between them. Tessy was leaning against her pink Barbie pillow her mom had sent her in a care package earlier that week. Timmy was stretched out on the floor, his head resting on his new Goosebumps pillow, with Sashi, Briana's golden retriever, head resting on his hip.

We watched *Bogus*, which was a story about a seven-year-old boy named Albert who lived in Las Vegas with his widowed mom, who suddenly died in an auto accident. Albert was sent to live with his mom's foster sister in New Jersey, a woman he'd never met before. Albert was despondent over the loss of his beloved mother and didn't like his new aunt much. Gerard Depardieu played his imaginary friend, a French magician named Bogus. Bogus helped Albert come to terms with his mother's death, eventually transitioning him into his new life with his aunt.

After the movie was over, Briana turned to me and said, "Hey, Auntie, Tessy's crying."

"What's the matter, Princess? Why are you crying?" I asked, as I stood up and walked over towards her.

"I don't want my mommy to die," she replied. Her eyes were filled with tears.

"Oh, Princess, your mommy's not going to die," I said, sitting on the arm of the chair, rubbing her back. I leaned over and kissed the top of her head.

"Auntie?" said Timmy.

"Yeah?"

"I don't want Mom to die either," he said, with watery eyes. His chin was tucked in under his pillow. He was fighting back tears.

Briana stood up, walked over to the sofa, and cuddled up next to Susan.

"Oh, come here, Timmy," I said, patting a small vacant spot on the cushion as I moved from the arm of the chair to the cushion next to Tessy.

Timmy crawled over my legs and slipped under the fleece blanket with Tessy. As the heavy rain pounded on the rooftop, we sat together, my arms cradling the kids while they cried for their mommy.

Our nightly bedtime ritual consisted of story time, lullabies, and prayers. For Christmas we received Shel Silverstein's, *Where the Sidewalk Ends*, a book of poems Timmy proudly recited from almost nightly. As I tucked the two of them into bed that evening, we said *double special* prayers for their mommy to get well. After I kissed each of them goodnight, just before I turned out the light, Tessy said, "Wait a minute, Auntie," as she leaned toward the nightstand, grabbing the floral picture frame of her mom. She placed the picture on top of her chest, wrapped her arms around it, and turned over onto her side facing the wall. She yawned and then whispered, "Good night, Mommy. I love you. I hope you get better very soon," before I turned out the lights. They reminded me of my own longing for my mother and realization that I still needed her, even though I hated to admit it.

Before the holidays, Steve and I talked on the phone. He had heard the kids and I were spending Christmas in Los Angeles and called to ask if he could take the kids to the Santa Monica Pier for an afternoon. I was torn. I'd heard he was in a new relationship. Even though the kids didn't have a deep bond with Steve, they liked him a lot, especially Timmy. Eventually I agreed to let the kids go because I wanted the kids to see that even though relationships end, there doesn't have to be a lot of unpleasantness around the situation. I wanted them to see that Steve and I could remain friends. But when they returned from the pier, Steve and I exchanged heated words. My big mistake was that I couldn't admit to myself that we weren't friends; we were barely on speaking terms with one another, or at least I with him.

One of the things he had said when he dropped the kids off that lingered for days, even weeks to come was, "You're just like your mother, you know. You're bitter and angry. And now you're alone raising the kids, the same way your mother did because your father didn't want to be around her."

Even though I wasn't on speaking terms with my mother, I didn't keep her from talking with her grandchildren. They had lived with her years ago, when they were babies, before Dad bought my sister her house. There was a special bond between Timmy, Tessy, and their nana that my mother didn't have with any of her other grandchildren. The kids loved her, and she absolutely adored them. I knew she missed the kids tremendously. She called them every couple of weeks and sent cards on special occasions. Our phone conversations were most often awkward and strained. "Hi Laura, it's Mum. Are the children there?" was all she'd say. When I heard her voice on the other end, I always felt a tightening in my body and a lump in my throat. Sometimes my teeth would clench. Once I noticed during one of those brief unexpected telephone encounters, I almost stretched out the entire phone cord because I was so tense.

The Saturday morning after the movie, I sat at my desk and *I* made the call. I wrapped my legs tightly around the legs of the chair while nervously tapping a pencil on the desktop. I even picked up the receiver, pushed the first few buttons of her phone number, and hung up before I actually made the real call. I swallowed my pride, but I knew it was something I had to do.

"Hi, Mom, it's Laura. Do you want to talk with the kids?" I asked.

"Oh, yes. Thank you," she replied.

"If it's okay, I'd like to share something funny that happened with the kids." I didn't wait for her response because I was afraid she'd say no, so I quickly continued, "The other morning while the kids and I were in bed, Timmy was on one side of me and Tessy was on the other side."

"Tessy said, 'We're like a sandwich.'"

"So I asked her, 'What kind of sandwich?'"

"Then she said, 'My favorite, a Marshmallow Fluff sandwich.'"

"I said to her, 'I remember Marshmallow Fluff. They still make that stuff?'"

"Then she said, 'Oh yes, Auntie! And Nana makes the best Marshmallow Fluff sandwiches in the whole wide world.'"

Then I said to my mom, feeling somewhat nostalgic, a little nervous, but mostly vulnerable, "It reminded me of the many times I came home from school, and you'd make me a Marshmallow Fluff sandwich. I remember how you used to cut off the crusts and slice the sandwich into four little triangles."

She didn't say a word.

With a dry mouth, I continued, "You know Mom, I'm sure by now you've heard that Steve and I are no longer engaged."

"Yes, I know," she said in a cool tone.

"I've been raising the kids pretty much on my own. It's made me realize that in many ways you raised us alone. I remember how Dad was never around. I see now that it was *you* who held our family together."

There was an uncomfortable pause.

"Well, thank you, Laura," she replied. There was another long pause, before she added, "You know, I'm a mother, and all I ever really wanted was for your father to be home every night with me and our family. I wanted a family man. I didn't want a husband who spent his life gambling, drinking, and God knows what else. Sure he got sober, but he gave up the lesser of the two evils. He had a gambling problem and by the time I realized it, it was too late." She sounded bitter. She took a long drag from her cigarette, then exhaled slowly making a soft hissing sound, before she said, "I try not to dwell on things, but I live with a lot of regrets. I did the best I could under the circumstances, and you need to know that."

Curiously, I asked, "But didn't you know he liked to gamble when you first met him?"

"I thought I could change him."

I asked solemnly, "So why didn't you leave him?"

"I couldn't," she said.

"Why?"

She was quiet for a moment and then said faintly, "I didn't feel I had any other options." She took another long drag from her cigarette, before a silence filled the space.

Suddenly I realized that's what I wanted too, to be a family with Steve, Timmy, and Tessy. And in a way, I felt bonded to her again, in our hurts and disappointments, and in the longing and bitterness we shared.

# After School

B ack in October, Timmy asked me if he could join the after school recreation program at his elementary school. The focus of the program was to provide supervised social play-based activities for kids.

"All the other boys in my class are going. Can I *please* join? *Please*?" he begged, while driving home from school one day.

Peering at Tessy in the rearview mirror, I asked, "Do *you* want to join too, Tessy?"

She rolled her eyes and gazed out the window, replying, "No. It's stupid. I don't wanna go."

"It's not *stupid*!" shouted Timmy, lurching at her from the front seat. Then he hollered, "What does she know anyway, she's just a *girrrrl.*" He turned back around and pleaded again, "Can I *please* go, Auntie, *please*?"

"Maybe. Let me check into it," was all I said.

I was learning to be careful making promises to them. I had found myself more than once saying "yes," then reneging because I hadn't explored all the options. I tried as best I could not to give them mixed messages. Though I later learned from Timmy that my "maybe" was more of a sure thing because, as he said, "Most times 'maybe' ended in 'yes.'"

For a couple of days I mulled over the advantages and disadvantages of Timmy attending the rec program. The main disadvantage was that every day I'd have to drive four miles down to school, pick Tessy up, bring her back home, then three hours later, drive back down again, get Timmy, and then bring *him* back home. What appealed to me was that Timmy would be given the chance to play organized sports like soccer, baseball, and kickball, every day. I figured it would do him a lot of good to run around, spinning his boundless energy by tumbling with other boys. He liked to play rough and tough sometimes.

For an hour every Saturday morning, he was glued to the TV watching wrestling matches. Mostly he loved watching Hulk Hogan, whose ring name was "The Super Destroyer." I didn't like him watching that stuff, but he insisted, arguing the point that he had been allowed to watch it since he was a little boy.

"Besides," he said, "I've had to give up so many things to move to California, like my school, my little league, and my best friend Ryan."

I couldn't argue with his reasoning, but I did try to monitor his behavior. Most often when he had finished watching the wrestling program, he went looking for the girls; he wanted someone to spar with. Once I witnessed him hand Tessy his soft yellow Wiffle bat and say, "Here, you can use this, and I'll just use my bare hands."

Tessy hit the bat away and said, "*No*, I *don't* want to fight. It's *stupid*. Leave me alone."

"Dang it, Tessy. *Please*," he begged.

"No!" she shouted back, before she walked away.

Another reason to support Timmy's request to go to the after school program was that Tessy wanted, actually she needed, alone time with me, every day. She still didn't like leaving my side much. She loved our simple routines like grocery shopping, going to the post office, shopping at the mall, or visiting the library. Timmy was often bored or jumpy when we ran errands. The truth was, I favored Tessy. I felt the soft, little girl inside me come alive when I was with her. She loved me mothering her, while Timmy resisted my affections most times. More than once, Timmy told me, "I'm a boy, and I'm too old for that mushy stuff." My favoring Tessy wasn't deliberate, it just happened over time. I hated myself for not wanting Timmy with me. I felt a private sorrow inside, feeling like an awful parent not wanting him around.

But by the time I called the school to register Timmy for the program it was already full.

Just before the Christmas school break, the school secretary called to say they had an opening. It was also around that time when the kids received their first report card. Timmy's teacher, Miss Johnson, wrote in the comments section, "Timmy is bright and intelligent, but doesn't always listen and is easily distracted because of his need for social contact. He cares for and likes helping others." I was convinced that the rec program was a way for him to get the extra social contact he needed.

According to Mr. Andrews, Tessy's teacher, he wrote, "Tessy is strong in the arts, especially music. But she's very shy and lacks self-esteem."

I asked Tony, our therapist, for some suggestions on how to use my alone time with Tessy to help build her confidence. He recommended, "Try to help her develop a positive concept of herself. Be generous with praise and words of encouragement. And, if you need to criticize her, do it in a way she understands it's about her behavior, not her." He also advised me to teach her to make positive statements about herself. Most of all, he said, "Help her to feel loved and wanted."

Timmy's attendance at rec immediately made a positive impact on *all* our lives. When I gave Tessy a few hours of special time, such as going to the coffee shop and sharing a muffin, or lingering in a toyshop playing and pretending, she was visibly happier. She cried less for her mommy and didn't knock on my bedroom door late at night scared and lonely, wanting to sleep with me. And Timmy was easier to be around because he had lots of "boy time," which was often the topic of conversation during dinner. I too was happier, finally understanding what it meant for a parent to be happy when their children are content and happy.

Late one Monday afternoon while Tessy was in the schoolhouse playing with Briana and I was preparing dinner, the telephone rang.

It was Mrs. Rinkus, the school secretary. "Your son Timothy's been injured. He's okay. But we think you should come get him right away."

"What happened? He's all right, isn't he?" I asked anxiously, drying my hands with a dishtowel.

"Don't worry, he's okay. A fifth grader was picking on a first grader, and Timothy jumped in trying to protect the younger boy. While running from the older boy, Timothy ran into a wall and hurt his shoulder. He's complaining about it, so we think it's best you come and get him," she explained.

I hung up and called Susan right away to let her know what had happened and asked her to watch Tessy. In a sudden state of panic, I grabbed my car keys and drove like a madwoman down the mountain. When I reached the electric gate entrance, I turned quickly onto the main road, and picked up speed, maneuvering my way through wooded hairpin turns.

Just as I reached the open road, two deer jumped out in front of me. Quickly, I tightly gripped the steering wheel with both hands and slammed on the brakes, steering the car straight ahead as I held my breath. I didn't hit either of the deer; they dashed off into the woods untouched. But out of nowhere, I caught a faint glimpse of a third baby deer. I continued pressing my foot hard and heavy on the brake, but couldn't stop in time. I smashed right into her, head on. The car came to a screeching halt, and the fawn fell onto the road.

I sat in the car, stunned and then screamed, "Shit!" while smacking the palm of my hands against the steering wheel. I held my breath while gripping the wheel tighter, as I peered over the front windshield. The fawn lifted her head, blinked her big brown eyes at me, jumped up onto her four legs, and dashed off into the woods behind her two other companions. I could hear the clicking hooves against the pavement and the thumping of my own heartbeat. I hung my head down, placed my forehead on top of the steering wheel, and started to cry.

Then I remembered Timmy.

I picked him up and brought him back to the house. He complained that his shoulder and collarbone hurt. Wendy, Michael, and Susan took a look at him, and all of us agreed he was fine. "Bruised," we concurred. The following day he was back in school running and climbing. He even played kickball during his after school program. He continued to move at his active pace during the day, but at night, when he took a bath or was getting ready for bed, he complained about his shoulder.

"It's just a bad bruise, honey. It's going to take time to heal," I told him.

"Shouldn't I see a doctor? Mom would take me to the doctor."

"I'm sure it's only a bruise," I said, trying to convince him.

As the week progressed, Timmy continued to play hard,

but in the quiet hours his complaints persisted. By Thursday night Susan suggested I take him to the doctor. So on Friday, four days after his accident, I took him to the doctor after school. The doctor placed his left arm in a sling and told me he had actually broken his collarbone!

For the longest time Timmy kept saying to me, "You didn't believe me, Auntie. I was telling you the truth, but you didn't believe me."

I felt terrible and hated myself. Mostly I hated motherhood.

# Being Somebody

The kids loved visiting L.A. What kid wouldn't? Every trip was an unbearably exciting adventure. During one of our monthly excursions, we visited Disneyland, where Tessy, who wore a knee-length pink and white polka-dot dress, got to meet and hug Minnie Mouse. She could hardly contain herself when Minnie Mouse held out her white gloved hand and twirled her around a couple of times. I shot an entire roll of film of her hugging Minnie Mouse, telling her over and over again how much she loved her.

We also visited Universal Studios, Knott's Berry Farm, and the Los Angeles Zoo. It didn't take long for us to create our rituals of visiting Puzzle Zoo at Santa Monica's Third Street Promenade and Sparky's Frozen Yogurt Shop on Main Street, where the kids experimented with every flavor until they found their favorite. We even carried our bicycles on the bike rack on the back of our wagon and cycled the Venice Beach bike path, stopping to watch break-dancers, bodybuilding muscle competitions, and volleyball games. Once, we even caught the tail end of a sand-sculpting exhibit.

On one particular Sunday afternoon while the kids were playing at the Venice Beach playground, Timmy found a five-inch black scorpion. He picked up a stick and started poking at it. My friend Rick assured him, and me, it was just a plastic toy. Rick picked it up by its long tail and threw it at Timmy. I swear Timmy jumped three feet into the air in a state of fright. Once he was certain it was just a toy, Timmy picked up the bug and walked around the playground showing all the little kids his latest find.

In late February, we drove down to Los Angeles to celebrate Timmy's ninth birthday.

Tessy, who was sitting behind me in the back seat, asked, "Auntie, can you *please* tell us a story about our mom when she was little." She loved hearing tales of how her mom had played the violin when she was her age, or that Joan carried her favorite doll, Mrs. Beasley, with her everywhere she went. She loved the story of when her mom was five years old and twirled a baton in the Memorial Day parade, fumbling in her attempts to spin it in her little inexperienced hands.

"I remember one afternoon our family drove to Aunt Elaine's house for a birthday party for our cousin Diane," I began.

"Do we know her?" asked Tessy.

"No, you've never met her, or my Aunt Elaine, who'd be your Great Aunt Elaine," I replied. "They lived on a lake. Most of the day we spent in the water, swimming, snorkeling, and boating. Your mom was around three years old. She wore a bright yellow one-piece skirted bathing suit with bold pink and lime-green love flowers."

"What are *love* flowers?" asked Tessy.

"It's a flower design from the sixties," I answered.

"Your mom had to go to the bathroom. She and your nana walked hand and hand back to Aunt Elaine's house. When they returned, just before they reached the concrete landing near the edge of the lake, your mom sat down on the stone walkway and peeled off her swimsuit. Your nana told her to put it back on, but your mom didn't listen to her. Instead, she ran quicker than a bunny up the hillside, onto the freshly seeded lawn, and stopped at the copper birdbath. She stood there tapping her little fingers playfully in the water. There was a tin bucket leaning against the base of the birdbath with three, maybe four long-stemmed artificial red roses. Your mom picked up one of the roses, placed it in her mouth, clenching the stem tightly between her teeth." I was stealing glances at Tessy from the rear-view mirror, who by now was leaning in closer to me, almost hugging the back of the front seat, smiling enthusiastically.

"What was she doing?" she asked.

"Just posing. She looked like a red haired flamenco dancer, clenching that rose in between her teeth, with one hand on her hip, and the other hand holding the stem of the rose."

"Then what happened?"

"Everyone started laughing. Uncle Dick grabbed the Polaroid and snapped a picture of her."

"What's a Polaroid?" asked Timmy from the back seat.

"It's a type of camera that develops pictures within seconds."

"Your nana still has that photo," I said, shaking my head, feeling amusingly reminiscent. I could tell Tessy was filled with giant joy.


One of the reasons Timmy was eager for this particular trip was that he wanted to capitalize on the celebration of his ninth birthday. My friends really liked the kids and made a big deal when we visited them. That entire weekend was jammed packed with a visit to the arcade, go-cart riding, plus rollerblading along the Strand. My friends Don and Ana hosted Timmy's birthday party, where he received lots of great gifts.

When we arrived back in Santa Cruz, we celebrated Timmy's birthday the following Saturday with his school buddies at the local roller rink. His actual birthday was on Sunday, the following day. So we gathered on Sunday morning with our extended family, along with Timmy's best friend, Brandon, who stayed over the night before, for *another* birthday celebration.

Before we sat down for breakfast, Michael, who was standing near the refrigerator, said to Timmy, "Hey, Timmy, come on over here a minute. I have something for you."

Panting and shaking his hands uncontrollably, Timmy replied, "What? What is it? What do you have for me?"

"Stand right here," said Michael, positioning him in front of the oven, arms length from him.

"Okay," said Timmy, who by now was bouncing and wiggling and going crazy with anticipation.

"Now close your eyes."

"Okay, okay," said Timmy, as he grinned and squeezed his eyes shut.

"And open your mouth."

Laughing, Timmy said, "Ahhh," with his hands jiggling by his sides.

Michael pulled out from behind his back a can of whipped cream and shot a wad of white foam into Timmy's mouth, filling it completely. With a twinkle in his eyes, Timmy just stood there laughing, unable to say a word or close his mouth. It was such a riot. A huge laughter filled the room.

After all the celebrations were over, I wondered to myself, *was it too much?* Timmy was very pleased with it all. I felt warm and happy inside because he felt so loved and acknowledged by many. But I was beginning to wonder if I was trying to overcompensate for the guilt and sadness I felt for his broken life—or maybe it was my own.

While in L.A., Shirley had asked me, "Do you miss your life here? Do you miss your career?"

My mind lingered as I began to think about the road I had traveled in such a short time. College life started at a local junior college where I entered into the psychology program. I wanted to be a child psychologist and work with kids. During my first semester, I volunteered at a local daycare center as a part-time teacher's aide. For the first time I could truthfully say I came face to face with underprivileged children. Mostly I remember two little girls, twins, who were around four years old. Every day my heart was pierced with sadness by their noticeable neglect. They showed up every morning, oftentimes late, with their shoulder length honey-blonde hair uncombed and snots running down their unwashed faces. It was common for them to wear the same soiled clothes days in a row. They were dirty, scrawny, and smelled of urine and spoiled milk. They were quiet, shy, and huddled together most of the time, barely interacting with the other children. They sought attention from us, their teachers. They wanted to be hugged and preferred sitting in our laps rather than playing with the other children.

Their need to be nurtured and cared for was more than I could handle at that time in my life. It would be years later before I understood I hadn't yet developed the emotional capacity to witness and be with their needs. I was so overwhelmed by it all, that when I went back to school after the summer break, I changed my major to business and began pursuing a professional career, climbing the corporate ladder as they say. But no matter how many hours I gave to my job, or how much attention I dedicated to a world of numbers and rational thinking, there was always a place inside me that felt empty, lonely, and lost.

Oriah Mountain Dreamer has a wonderful line in her poem titled, *The Invitation,* "I want to know if you can be alone with yourself and if you truly like the company you keep in the empty moments." I spent so many years trying to be somebody, somebody other than who I was. I didn't see that maybe I was trying to prove something. But to whom? I was looking outside myself. Ultimately I could say the struggle was within me.

One day while at church, the theme of the day was "Self." While standing at the podium, our minister, Sandy, said, "At the end of one's life, some people know others more than they know themselves."

I'd never really thought much about knowing and understanding myself. But when I started taking care of the kids, it was evident to me that I had been taken back into childhood, revisiting my early life, feeling the errors of childhood I had tried so hard to leave behind. It was through parenting that I learned how my unresolved childhood losses and longings continued to influence my present day adult life. While parenting the kids, I was learning how to parent myself and how to find my way home, back to my true self. Love is like that you know. Loving the kids made me want to look deep inside myself for the answers and the truth. I wanted to give them the very best of me. I didn't ever want to forget the important things. They opened a door and no matter what, I wanted to face everything with love.

# Why Not Motherhood?

The months of rain and wet fog finally lifted and spring was once again making its appearance. Bright yellow daffodils and golden California poppies were beginning to cover the grassy hillsides. It was the first warm day we'd seen in the Bay Area in months. The kids and I decided to drive to Natural Bridges State Beach to watch the seals and otters and to idle in wonderment at the tide pools. As we were getting ready, Tessy walked into my room, almost tiptoeing, with her hands delicately cupped together.

Teary eyed, she said, "Auntie, my cross necklace broke, the one Mommy gave me for my birthday. She said it would keep me safe and protect me. But it's broken. Can you fix it, *please*?"

"Sure, Princess. Come on over here," I said, sitting at my desk, motioning her with a wave of my hand.

"Ouch!" she shrieked and began hobbling around on one foot

Turning my head back toward her, I said, "What happened?"

"I stubbed my toe on that *stupid* carpet," she replied, hopping her way closer toward me with the necklace chain dangling from her still cupped hands. She stood in front of me and opened her hands, showing me the broken silver cross with a single red ruby, her birthstone, in the center. Tears were dripping down her face. I picked her up, sat her on my lap, and cradled her as she cried in my arms while she held tightly onto the cross.

A few moments later, she looked up at me with her red nose and puffy eyes and said, "Auntie, I'm having a bad day today."

Silently I chuckled as I wiped her wet cheeks. I kissed her face and head over and over as I held her close, rocking her, wondering why it was I didn't have children of my own.

Ever since early adulthood, I had thought, *one day* I'll have children. But that *one day* never seemed to come. I met Billy, my former husband, when I was sixteen. We fit together like two pieces of a jigsaw puzzle. He had a smooth, dark face, long ringlet hair the color of mid-night sky, and huge dark eyes. From the moment we met, we hated being apart from one another. He was my best friend and I knew early on, when I was just a teenager, that I'd marry him one day.

We married when I was twenty-three and agreed we'd have a baby and start our family when Billy turned thirty and I twenty-seven. We figured by then we'd have spent a few years settling into our careers, bought a home, saved some money, and have a few adventures under our belt so we wouldn't feel like we had missed out on the things young couples liked do. One night, months prior to Billy's thirtieth birthday, I cried in his arms, telling him I wasn't ready to have a baby just yet.

"What's going on, Babe?" he asked.

"I'm only twenty-seven and want to live life. There's so much I haven't done yet," I told him.

"Yeah. But we can spend our entire life saying that."

"I feel like I'm just too young. We have plenty of time for parenthood, later, maybe in a few years. But I can't now. I just can't," I cried.

"What are you afraid of?" he asked.

"I'm not *afraid* of anything. It's just, well, not the right time yet." I offered him a consolation prize—a motorcycle of his choice—another toy with promises of road trips we dreamed of taking some day. He was okay with it; he just wanted me to be happy. But as time moved on, anytime *that* discussion came around, my response remained the same, "In a few years."

It wasn't like we had a fight or anything. After we moved to California, something changed. Call it a mid-marriage crisis, or maybe it was the seven-year itch. A door opened, and I entered it, and a distance crept in which made me begin to reexamine my life and the choices I had made. I loved my husband, but for the first time since we had met twelve years earlier, I began to question my need for independence and ultimately, my commitment to him. In time, he met and married a woman who gave him the children and lifestyle he truly wanted.

I sat on the beige suede tub chair with my hands folded in my lap, staring at the children's play area in Tony's office one late morning.

I looked over at Tony and asked, "What's wrong with me?"

"What do you mean?" he replied, sitting relaxed across from me in the matching chair with a white notepad resting on his lap.

"I think I've been afraid of motherhood all these years."

"Do you want to say more?"

"Well, you know I've had an estranged relationship with my mother since I was a teenager, maybe even before then."

"Yes," he answered, nodding his head.

"I spent years being angry with her and adamant I didn't want to be like her. I think all this time I've been afraid I'd end up just like her. I thought my reason for not having children was because I had a choice, as a woman. My drive in the business world, I thought, was based on the idea that I'm one of the first generations of women who actually *had* a choice. I didn't *have* to get married, have babies, and be dependent on anyone. At least that's what I told myself. But now I wonder. I wonder if my decision not to embrace motherhood was because I was afraid I'd be like her."

Welling with sadness, I took a long pause.

"But the truth is, I see so much of her in me. It scares me. As time passes, I find myself more and more like her, in the way I sip a cup of tea, or the giddiness I feel over the holidays. I see her when I stare at my hands, they're like hers, long and thin, or in the arch of our brows." I looked over at the children's play table and said, "The thing is, what I feared most has come true."

"What's that?"

"Well, I'm alone, like her. And I'm angry, even resentful, just like her. The other day, while I was preparing dinner, one of the rivets on my belt got caught on the drawer handle and tore the belt, so I took it off. I told Timmy to put it in the Goodwill bag. Timmy told me, 'No, Auntie. You can still use it like Nana does to hit us when we're bad.' I couldn't believe I had heard him say that. I probed him a bit and learned that their grandmother hit them regularly with a belt on their hands when they did something wrong. I got so triggered. First of all, she used to hit me with a belt, and I hated her for doing that. All sorts of memories began to flood me. They're only little children! I got so angry with my mother. But later, after I put the kids into bed, while I was journaling, I remembered that I too hit them, you know, that time in Hawaii. It makes me so sad and angry. I hate my mother, yet I see her in me, too." I leaned over and grabbed a few tissues as tears ran down my face.

After I cried for some time, Tony explained, "We all have childhood wounds. Parenting can sometimes offer us an opportunity to heal those wounds, to develop understanding, empathy, even forgiveness when we see ourselves in our parent's shoes. Ultimately it all comes back to us. It's *our* pain. It's *our* suffering. When we are present with our suffering, or feel our imperfections, rather than denying our pain or berating others or ourselves with judgment or criticism, we begin to understand ourselves through self-compassion. Self-compassion is about caring for ourselves, being kind and understanding when confronted with personal failings or accepting our humanness."

I thought about the years of discord between my mother and I. I thought about all the anger and rage I felt toward her, all the bitterness I had running around in my head. Even though she was not the woman I wanted to be, she existed in me. In the course of my wanderings, in the search for my own identity, separate from hers, I came to see how I denied a part of her that lived inside myself; her lonely shadow had been there all along.

# A Time For Celebration

Easter Sunday was a full-on celebration at the house. Wendy, Michael, and Susan hosted a luncheon for their friends, with a jazz trio playing a mixture of pop classics and ragtime. The festivities officially began at noontime in the meadow with the opening of the new in-ground trampoline. We gathered in a huge circle around the trampoline while everyone, both young and old, took turns jumping. At one point there must've been a dozen people, mostly kids, bouncing together. Michael also hired an Easter bunny to entertain us all. She showed up wearing a ruffled paisley apron and carried a large white wicker basket with woven pastel colored ribbons. Her arrival commenced an Easter egg hunt for almost twenty kids.

The night before, Timmy, Tessy, Briana, and I had sat at the dining room table with candy piled high on two huge oval silver platters. They were full of excitement and talked non-stop as we filled over two hundred plastic colored eggs with M&M's, jellybeans, robin's eggs, and Hershey's Kisses. Susan and Wendy had the task of hiding them the following morning before guests arrived.

We dressed in our finest for the occasion. I had taken the kids clothes shopping the weekend before. Tessy picked out an ankle-length coral and yellow shoulder-tie floral sundress and a matching yellow bonnet. Timmy's choice of a white pair of trousers wasn't necessarily practical, but he sure looked handsome when posing for pictures wearing a blue and white striped short-sleeved gauze shirt and a shiny new black leather belt. For Christmas Susan had bought all three kids plush animal slippers, which they wore during the egg hunt.

My friend Kate drove up from Los Angeles to visit her family in San Francisco for the holiday weekend and stopped by for a few hours with gifts for the kids.

"Wow, cool! Thank you, Kate," said Timmy, unwrapping a Gushing Grape Bubble Tape. It was a round plastic container, about the size of a hockey puck. It looked like a tape dispenser.

"What? You gave the kids six feet of gum! What're you thinking?" I passed her a curt look.

"Um, sorry," she replied, looking apologetic. "Isn't that what you give kids on Easter? It's what I gave my brother's kids and nobody seemed to mind."

"Cool. Look, Auntie. I got cotton candy flavor," said Tessy, looking quite pleased as she gave Kate a warm hug before adding the gum to her already full Easter basket.

"Well, would you want *your* kids eating six feet of gum?" I asked Kate.

"*Well*, that's probably why *I* don't have kids," she answered, smirking back at me.

Back at the house, where lunch was being served, I decided to have a glass of chardonnay. It was a rare occasion. I had spent years overdrinking, mostly in my twenties, but had stopped a number of years back. I got tired of that hangover feeling the next day and noticed it was taking longer for me to recover from a night of drinking. The kids had never seen me drink before. I was standing outside on the patio, next to the bar one of the house staff had set up. It was a long fold-up table covered with a couple of neatly pressed white linen tablecloths. On one end of the table were lilac floral paper cups, matching napkins, and a stainless steel ice bucket with an assortment of juices, water, and soda. On the other end were bottles of opened and unopened wine, plus a couple of dozen Crate & Barrel wine glasses, and a stack of purple cocktail napkins. In the middle of the table sat a large white and lavender orchid.

I was talking with Kate and Eric, a friend of Michael's, when Eric asked if he could pour me a glass of wine. Timmy walked onto the patio as Eric handed me the glass.

Timmy rushed over to me and asked, "What are you drinking?"

"I'm having a glass of wine," I announced, holding my glass up to the sun.

"No!" he yelled. "You can't do that! You'll die!" He gripped his forehead with his hand.

I chuckled. "It's okay, Timmy," I said, reaching my free hand out to pat his shoulder.

"No!" he argued, as he took a step back and stomped his foot. "You'll die! Then who'll take care of us?" He wrinkled his face into a scowl and shrugged his shoulders. He began pacing anxiously.

"It's just *one* glass of wine. Don't worry. It's okay. I'm not going to die."

He folded his hands together in front of his chest as he walked toward me. "*Please*, Auntie. *Please*, don't drink alcohol. You'll die. *Please*." His eyes were beginning to water.

"Okay, I won't drink it," I said and placed the glass on top of the bar.

I took a step toward him, extending my arm for him to come closer into me. He threw his arms around my waist and squeezed me tight, as he buried his face into my chest. I felt his fear and anguish as I recalled the scene of how he found his mom passed out on the living room floor drunk last summer after her stroke and how he thought she was dead. I took a deep breath in as I ran my hand through his short thick hair.

A moment later, he was gone, off to play with the other kids. Neither of us mentioned that alcohol incident again.

The following day was my thirty-fifth birthday. I decided to spend it alone. I dropped the kids off at school that morning and continued driving south on Route 1 for the one-hour drive to Carmel. Susan agreed to pick the kids up from school and take care of them until I returned the following afternoon. I checked into the Mission Ranch Farmhouse, a historical 1850s bed and breakfast Clint Eastwood had purchased in the eighties, rescuing it from a potential condominium development. He had had it completely renovated to match the styles of the original buildings. It was a sprawling property with several white farmhouses, a sheep-filled pasture, and sunset ocean views. I spent the day strolling the beach, walking the cobblestone streets, and visiting the quaint shops and art galleries.

Later in the evening, while reading a book in my room, with the wild wind howling outside my window, I drifted into slumber, then awoke, startled by a dream. In my dream I was with my best friend from junior high school, Gail Gilpatrick, though we were in present day time. We were driving down Pearl Street in Brockton, the street she lived on when we were kids. She was driving a pale yellow Mustang convertible with the top down. I was in the passenger's seat. As we cruised down the road, she told me she wanted to be "single, free, unattached, not tied down to anything." I was torn. I wasn't sure I wanted to raise the kids any longer and began questioning if I should live a carefree life, just like her. I finally made the decision to live the single life and was amused and happy for just a short time. Then a deep loneliness crept in. I began missing the kids very much. I remembered thinking in my dream, *How can I teach the kids we're here to help and care for one another, if I don't help and care for them?* When I awoke from my dream, I felt terribly lonely—lost inside myself, wishing I was home with the kids. I missed them fiercely. In a state of anxiety, I called Susan to check on them.

"They had a good day today. They were happy and went to bed without a problem. So don't worry, Auntie. Enjoy your solitude," she told me.

I closed my eyes, but I couldn't sleep. My mind was stirred by the dream, by my torment of wanting both my freedom and family life.

The next morning I arose early and took a long walk along the beach. Eventually I found my way over to the Carmel Mission. San Carlos Borromeo de Carmelo Mission, a Roman Catholic mission church founded in 1771, was one of the twenty-one religious and military outposts established in California by Spanish Catholics to spread the Christian faith among the local Native Americans. I took a tour of the five mission museums, ending at The Basilica Church.

I sat alone on the dark wooden pew in the back of the church. In the midst of the serenity, a thin golden light trickled into the church while tourists made their way silently along the center aisle. The sweet exotic fragrance of pink-ladies and Easter lilies filled the air, as dozens of the trumpet shaped flowers sat around the altar. I stared up at the curved walls forming a parabolic arch, thinking about life's twists and turns, wondering how I had come to be in my current life. I smiled at the thought of being a mother, or at least the form of motherhood I was currently experiencing. The joys and sorrows of parenthood engulfed me, yet I felt happy to be living such an incredible experience. My thoughts turned to the previous week, when Tessy and I had started singing "Too-Ra-Loo-Ra-Loo-Ra," an Irish lullaby we had learned from Briana. At bedtime, after stories and prayers, we would gaze deeply into each other's eyes as we sang the lyrics in perfect harmony.

My heart felt so overjoyed by the gift of loving and being loved. I now had a family to care for and cherish and love in my heart. I realized I'd become a better person when forgetting myself and caring for others. While sitting in the church, I remembered the dream I had had the night before, and my happiness gave way to a deep fear and sadness inside. I grew weary as I began to wonder, *how on earth could I imagine my life without them?* Thoughts turned to my future, our future, and the possibility of losing them.

# Who's in Control?

It was Friday evening. Tessy was sleeping at Briana's house for the night. After bedtime stories and prayers, I told Timmy, "I have a headache, and I'm not feeling well. So *please*, make sure you don't wake me up until after eight. Okay?"

"What? But that's late!" he grumbled.

"I know, but tomorrow's Saturday. You can sleep in."

"I don't wanna sleep in," he argued, turning over onto his side. "Can I go up to the kitchen?"

"No. I don't want you waking Wendy or Michael up either."

"Can I go down to Susan's house and play with the girls?"

"No. I don't want you interrupting their girl time. You can hang out here in your room, quietly. You can play with your Game Boy," I told him, as I leaned over and kissed him on the cheek before I turned out the lights.

I knew I'd be up half the night tossing and turning with cramps because I had my menses. Every so often I was plagued by painful cramps and nothing seemed to relieve them. Soaking in a warm lavender bath helped a little. The best antidote I discovered was to get plenty of rest and slow my pace *way* down. I couldn't imagine the kids understanding what went on for me during that time of the month. It wasn't

like I was sick and needed to stay in bed. It was more like I
was on edge; I tended to be more moody and things seemed
to get on my nerves more easily. In general, life seemed to be
a bit more intense around that time.


The following morning there was a faint knock on my bedroom
door. It grew louder and louder, until finally, it woke me up
out of a dead sleep.

"What? Who? Who's there? Who's knocking?" I yelled,
startled.

"It's me, Auntie. It's Timmy." His voice sounded muffled,
as if his lips were pressed up against the other side of the
door.

"What?" I yelled again. I lifted my head off the pillow and
looked at the clock. It read 6:57. I let out a loud groan as my
head fell heavily back down onto the pillow.

"Auntie?" asked Timmy, his voice still muffled.

I took in a long, deep breath, tightly grabbed hold of the
bed sheets with both my hands, and tore them off my body.
With crazed, ferocious eyes, I forced myself up and out of
bed. My heels hit the floor with a heavy thump. I stomped
heftily across the wooden floor. With one hand bracing the
wall and the other pulling hard the cold metal doorknob, fast
and furiously I opened the door wide.

I screamed, "What do you want? I told you last night
not to wake me until eight, didn't I? Why are you waking me
up?"

Startled, he took a step back as he crouched his shoulders
almost to his ears. Crossing his arms in front of his chest, he
tightly grabbed hold of his elbows.

With downcast eyes, he said, "I, I can't sleep. I'm hungry.
I want some breakfast."

Red-faced, I grabbed him by the hand, pulled him into

his room, over to his bed, and then pointed for him to get back into it.

"And now, since you didn't listen to me, you're in bed until ten!" I shouted, still pointing for him to climb back into bed. "Don't even *think* about trying to get out before that time! Got it?" I screamed, before I turned back around and stormed out of the room.

I heard his meek "Got it," before I slammed the door shut behind me.

I was that furious. I wasn't sure why I had gotten so angry. I knew at times he didn't listen. More than that, I knew he was a good boy who mostly did as I told him. I tried to understand his restlessness, his worry, his need for attention and contact. But at that moment, when he hadn't followed my directions, all I could see was red.


Not many days afterwards, we had our family therapy session with Tony. The first item on my list was to talk about that very incident. While the kids sat in the play area, I shared the story with Tony.

When I completed, Tony turned to Timmy and asked, "Timmy, do you have anything to say about what your Auntie just said?"

"Yes," he muttered, as he placed the racecar on top of the track.

"Okay. You have the floor," replied Tony, waving his hand like a maestro offering the spotlight to a performer.

Without taking his eyes off the racetrack, Timmy uttered, "Auntie is mean to us sometimes. She doesn't understand about being a kid. She just gets angry and mean."

I slouched back in my chair with my mouth hung open wide. Out of the corner of my eye I saw Tessy, who was kneeling in front of the dollhouse rearranging furniture, silently nodding her head in agreement. For days leading up to our therapy session, I wouldn't budge and held strong in my position that *Timmy* was in the wrong. It was *Timmy* who needed to work on controlling himself and his actions. It was *Timmy* who was the problem.

Feeling defeated, I turned to Tony and asked, "Is he right? *Am* I being mean? Is it *my* fault? Am *I* the problem?"

Tony placed his pen down and said, "It's not about who's to blame. It's not about finding fault. Perhaps that's your early childhood conditioning."

I gave him an odd look as I shook my head and shrugged my shoulders, letting him know I didn't know.

He continued, "If you can see that by focusing on yourself and your own reactions, instead of trying to force the kids to change so you can feel like you're 'in control', you'll learn and model for them, that external events—including other people's behavior—don't hold power over you."

Tony helped me to see how vital it was for me to take responsibility for my feelings and my actions. In the end, the anger I experienced was mine; it had nothing to do with the kids.

The morning after our therapy session, I dropped the kids off at school, ran a few errands, and returned home somewhere around eleven. While unpacking groceries, Wendy stepped into the kitchen. She and Michael had just returned late the night before from a trip to New York. We chatted for a few minutes, and then she told me Joan had called a couple of times while I was out. She said it was important, so I picked up the phone and called her back.

"Hi, Joan. It's me. You called?" I tucked the cordless phone in between my ear and shoulder as I stocked the pantry.

"I had my appointment with the neurologist this morning.

I want my kids back."

I stood frozen.

"What? I thought…"

"You thought what? I'm getting ready to complete the program. The year will be over in a couple of months. I want my kids back with me," she said firmly.

I was too stunned to respond.

"Did you hear me?"

"Yeah, I heard you," I replied, standing motionless. "Is Dad there? Can I talk with him?"

"This has nothing to do with Dad. He's not here. But just so you know, I'll do whatever I have to do to get my kids back. I want them back!" she commanded.

"Yep. I hear you," I said reluctantly. "Can you please tell Dad to call me?" I walked out of the pantry and into the kitchen. I felt dazed, alone amidst the scattered groceries and empty bags.

Wendy reentered the kitchen.

I"I just got off the phone with my sister."

"How's she doing?" she asked, pulling a mug off the shelf.

"She just saw her neurologist and wants the kids back soon."

Wendy closed the cabinet door, turned to me and asked, "How do you feel about that?"

I felt empty, lifeless, and numb. Everything seemed to slow down. I could feel the pulsation of my breath and the beating of my heart. The electric kettle whistled louder and louder before Wendy shut if off.

I looked at her bewildered and finally mumbled, "I don't want to give them up," before I walked out of the kitchen, leaving the groceries behind.

While walking to my bedroom, I passed Michael's

office.

He was sitting behind his desk and called out, "Hi Auntie."

I stopped, turned around, and poked my head into his office.

With a gloomy face, I said, "Welcome home."

"What's the matter?" he asked.

Standing in the doorway, I started to cry. He stood up and waved his hand for me to come into the room. I sat opposite him in the leather chair. He handed me a box of tissues as I proceeded to tell him the story.

He walked around the desk and gave me a big hug, saying, "What an incredible experience you've had parenting your sister's children. I'm sure it's difficult to imagine life without them. It sounds like your life might take you in a different direction soon."

"I don't want a different life. I want to be a family with Timmy and Tessy," I said sobbing.

"But, Auntie," he said, stroking my head gently. "You might not have a choice in the matter. Do you see the possibility that life maybe guiding you towards something else now?"

"I don't want anything else, I want to stay a family with them."

I made my way back to my room crying and noticed the kids' bedroom door was open. I entered it slowly and looked around the room. Timmy's green Goosebumps mask he had worn for Halloween lay on the floor next to the play table and the new Red Sox cap his mother had sent him sat on the corner of the wooden chair. Tessy's pink and purple string sun-catcher she'd made at school hung in the window and her markers, crayons, and sheets of song lyrics lay on top of her nightstand. I took a mental snapshot of their unmade beds, clothes and a bath towel hanging haphazardly on the wicker hamper, Tessy's new dance outfit folded neatly on top of their dresser, and Briana's four-foot shorthaired golden retriever stuffed animal leaning against the bunk-bed ladder.

I wanted to stay in that moment forever. I wanted time to freeze. I didn't want anything to change. I didn't want them, or us, or our family, to go away. I wanted to hold on to everything, exactly as it was, for as long as I could. Moments later, my phone rang. It was Dad.

Still crying, I asked him, "I thought you told me her therapist didn't think she was capable of taking care of the kids. Has that changed?"

"As I told you months ago, we weren't sure. This is news to me, too. I arrived home shortly after Joan called you, and she told me the same thing. I just got off the phone with her therapist. He said Joan's been working really hard these last few months and making great improvement. She's being evaluated to see if she's competent enough to take the kids back. If she is, they're going to work towards reunification."

"But Dad, I thought, I thought she wasn't going to get well. I thought I was going to take care of them, permanently," I said, as I wiped the tears from my face.

"I know, Laura," he said.

"I don't want to give them back."

"I know, dear. We just have to take it one day at a time. That's all we can do right now."

# Mother's Day

It was a hot Saturday afternoon in early May. The brilliant blue sky was the perfect backdrop for an afternoon pool party. The kids and I drove with Susan and Briana to Los Gatos to attend the fortieth birthday celebration for Robert, an old college friend of Susan's. He and his wife Patricia had three children, and Emilie, their youngest, was Tessy's age. Susan and I parked ourselves on a couple of navy blue cushion chaise lounges on the lawn close to the shallow end of the pool, where the kids played for hours.

Some time around mid-afternoon, Robert's two older boys strung a volleyball net in the pool. Each kid paired with an adult. Timmy teamed up with Andy, a short muscular middle-aged man who looked a bit like Jack LaLanne. In between volleyball games, Andy gave Timmy lots of attention, asking him questions like, "How old are you?" "Where do you go to school?" "What are your hobbies?" "Do you play sports?"

Timmy ate it up. He didn't give Andy the usual one-word answers. Instead, he elaborated on the details of his life. He told him about his mother's stroke and how up until the time he moved to Santa Cruz, he had been the man of the house and the oldest in his family. He also made it a point to let Andy know he had had the responsibility of looking out for his two younger sisters.

I smiled watching Timmy bask in Andy's attention. I was always delighted when a man took an interest in him. I sensed it was difficult for him not to have a dad, though he was optimistic enough and didn't talk about it much. Baseball was one of the greatest pleasures in Timmy's life. He knew lots about the players and stats and from all the years he had spent watching televised games, he could name the location of a ball field just by seeing the stadium on TV. He prided himself on that type of knowledge. Michael often told him, "You're an astute young man, Timmy." But the God-awful truth was, he couldn't hit or catch a baseball.

During one of his little league games he was playing the left fielder and when a ball came his way, he tripped and didn't catch the ball. All kids his age do those kinds of things, but he did them more than most kids. I knew in my heart he struggled with it. Every once in a while when he struck out or didn't catch a ball that should've been a sure thing, he hung his head low and moaned, "I suck." I believed he would've been a better player if he had had a dad throwing the ball to him, like some of his friends who were good at the sport. My dad had taken him to a few Red Sox games at Fenway Park when he was younger. He loved going to the stadium and was grateful for the experience, but he said to me one day, "It's not the same as my friends going with their dads." Mostly it was a silent kind of suffering he endured.

I watched on the sidelines as Andy and Timmy splashed around in the pool. Over and over again Andy crouched down into the water so Timmy could climb up onto his back and shoulders. Then Andy stood up and with Timmy holding onto his hands and would thrust him forward, up into the air, before Timmy dove down, splashing back into the water. They played and teased one another during the entire three volleyball games.

It was during the last game when Timmy and Andy made a bet on who'd score the winning point. It was clear who had won when Timmy shouted with elation, "I won, I won!" waving his arms victoriously while jumping and splashing up and down in the pool. Andy picked him up and carried him around on his broad shoulders like an Olympic hero. After his moment of glory, both of them stepped out of the pool, and Timmy followed Andy over to a bench near the food table. Moments later, Timmy came skipping toward me waving his left hand high up into the air.

As he came closer, he yelled, "Auntie, you don't ever have to worry again. I'm gonna take care of you from now on. Everything's going to be okay. I just won a million dollars!"

I looked up from my book and smiled. "Way to go, Timmy. Congratulations! Let's see it."

"You see," he said, grabbing each end of the bill with both hands, "it's a million dollars. Andy and I made a million-dollar bet, and I won! I scored the winning team point and won the bet!"

"Well done!" I turned and winked at Susan.

"You see, Susan, I won a million dollars!" he repeated. His body was still dripping wet.

"I see that Timmy. Congratulations! What are you going to do with all that money?" she asked, as she adjusted the brim of her hat to shade her eyes from the blinding sun.

Timmy turned toward me and said, "Well, first I'm gonna take care of my Auntie, and my mom, and Tessy and Lilly." He looked down and studied the bill hard for a long while.

He had a good heart. He cared about other people, more so than any other kid I ever met. I felt so moved, so proud when he shared his sincere intentions to take care of everyone with his newfound winnings. I looked over at Susan and gave her a warm smile as I stood up, placed a towel around his shoulders, and hugged him from behind. I didn't have the heart to tell him it was fake. I didn't want to spoil his moment.

While sitting in the passenger's seat of Susan's car later in the evening, I finally told him, "It's not real, Timmy," after he had talked endlessly on the drive home about what he was going to do with the money.

"It's *real*," he said, and shrugged his shoulders.

I turned around, looked him square in the eye, and said again, "Sorry, honey, it's not. I hate to burst your bubble, but it's not real."

"Yes it is! How do you know it's not?" he replied, still tightly clenching the bill.

"Timmy, there's no such thing as a million-dollar bill. Besides, a million dollars is a lot of money, right?"

"Well, yeah."

"Does it make sense a man, whom you don't even know, would bet you a million dollars, and give it to you?" I tried to appeal to his sensible side. I didn't want to disappoint him, but I also didn't want him thinking crazy thoughts about how he'd spend his money and be disappointed in a much bigger way later.

I finally let it go, when he muttered, "I don't care what you say. I know it's real."

The following morning was Mother's Day. I woke up some time around seven and noticed the kids' room was unusually quiet. *They're still sleeping*, I thought, so I lay in bed and journaled for half an hour or so. When I glanced at the clock, it was past 7:30, so I decided to go check on them. I put on my white fleece bathrobe and walked over to the door. Just as I opened the door a crack, I heard them walking down the hallway.

"Shhh, Tessy." said Timmy. "Remember, it's a surprise."

I quietly closed the door, crept back to bed, took off my robe, and climbed back into bed. A moment later there was a knock on the door.

"Come in," I said, sitting up in the bed with my journal by my side.

"Surprise! Happy Mother's Day!" they shouted, as they walked into the bedroom wearing huge, happy smiles.

Timmy was carrying a bamboo serving tray that contained an English muffin, a miniature jar of strawberry jam, and a bowl of grapes. There was a Valentine's Day mug that contained orange juice, though some had spilled onto the tray during the walk from the kitchen to my room. There was also a little periwinkle blue glass vase with a single pink rose hanging lopsided. Tessy, who crept along beside Timmy, carried a card and two gifts.

"For me? Oh, what a wonderful surprise! Thank you so much. I didn't even know about this. You *really* did surprise me, you know," I said, with a twinkly smile.

"We kept it a surprise for you," said Tessy. She hopped onto the end of the bed, crawling toward me with the card in her mouth and a gift in each hand.

Timmy placed the tray carefully next to me on the bed, walked around to the other side, and climbed on top. I leaned over and hugged and kissed them both. Tessy insisted I open my gifts first. Timmy gave me a red heart-shaped rock with tiny white hearts painted all over it.

"It was a school project. We had to look for a heart-shaped rock, and then we painted it," he said, as he took it from my hands. "See, feel it. It's heavy. You can use it as a paper weight if you want."

"It's beautiful! Thank you *so* much. I can put it on my desk to keep the papers from flying all over the room when it's windy." I leaned over and gave him a big kiss and hug.

"Now open my gift, Auntie," said Tessy, as she handed me a simple white box with pink and red heart stickers she had added herself.

She had made me a red Styrofoam heart with a smaller white Styrofoam heart inside it. Two blue velvet ribbons hung from the bottom, making it look like a heart medal. On the back she had cut and pasted two halves of a heart, one side out of pink construction paper and the other side out of red construction paper. She signed it in pencil, "To Mom, Love Tessy. I love you every day."

"Oh, Tessy, it's beautiful! I love you too. Thank you *so* much," I said, as I leaned over, kissing her all over her face.

"I didn't write 'To *Auntie*, Love Tessy' because since my mommy's not here with me, I wanted *you* to be my mommy today." She smiled and cuddled in closer next to me.

Tears of joy filled my eyes. Tessy never liked it when people called me her mommy. She insisted on letting them know, "She's my aunt!" It hadn't bothered me when it happened while I was back East visiting. But when I started caring for her, it was like a dagger in my heart every time I heard her say it. It didn't make much sense to me, why I wanted her to love me the way a daughter loves her mommy. But I longed for her in that way. It pleased me more than words could ever say, when she invited me to be her mommy on that very special day.

There was a five-foot potted fir tree sitting in the center of the altar when we arrived at church. While standing at the podium, our minister, Sandy, talked about how the deep-rooted system of trees is symbolic of our ancestral heritage. With a microphone in one hand and a red carnation in the other, she walked around the altar and talked about the different ways one honors their mother. Eventually she invited us to present our offerings, made in honor or memory of our own mothers, onto the tree.

Timmy, who was sitting next to Tessy, who was sitting next to me, leaned over and whispered, "Auntie, what's our offering?"

Leaning into Tessy, I replied, "We don't have one."

"Why not?" he asked.

"We didn't know we were supposed to bring an offering because we didn't go to church last weekend. Remember, we were in L. A.? Don't worry, it's okay that we don't have anything to share."

One by one members of the church took the microphone, stood near the tree, and shared their prayers, wishes, and stories about their beloved mother, as they placed their offering on or around the tree.

Timmy raised his hand, stood up, and said, "I have something I want to offer the church."

Startled, Tessy and I looked at each other, shrugged our shoulders simultaneously, and stared at Timmy.

Sandy spoke into the microphone, "Sure, Timmy. Come on up."

Timmy walked up to the altar, took the microphone in his hand, reached into his jean pocket, and pulled out his million-dollar bill.

He then said, "Yesterday, I won this million dollars. It means a lot to me. And I want to give it to the church, so you can do good things for people like my mom, who need help." He handed the microphone back to Sandy, walked over to the tree, and placed the million-dollar bill on top of one of the branches.

With admiring eyes, I watched him casually walk back to the bench, sit down, and give all his attention to the next person making an offering. I reached my hand over Tessy and patted Timmy's thigh, as tears of proud love drenched my heart.

# It'll All Work Out

**B**ack in September, Tessy began taking tap and ballet lessons once a week after school. For the first couple of months I didn't really have much of an interest hanging out with all the other mothers who watched and cheered their little ones on. My job was to get her to the studio and help her change into her little outfit. That's all. Once class started, I left. Timmy stayed in the car playing with his Game Boy because he "didn't want to stick around and watch a bunch of little girls dance." And frankly, neither did I. Every week on the drive home after class, Tessy would say, "But Auntie, I want you to *stay* and watch me like all the other mommies." I just shrugged it off because I felt I was already doing enough.

One day while I was helping Tessy change, Miss Gina, Tessy's dance teacher, asked me if I wanted to take a mothers' dance class. Tessy grabbed my arm, shook my purse, pleading with me, "Yes, Auntie, say 'yes,' *please*." But I didn't. I wasn't interested in watching little girls dance, let alone *learning* how to dance. But over time, I began to have a change of mind, or heart. After we settled into our new home, and the kids and I found our groove together, I was available to them in a more expanded way. As I let them more into my heart, I had a natural desire and interest in watching Tessy dance. In time, I became one of those doting mothers sitting on the long hard wooden bench lovingly admiring the successes and foibles of my little girl.

Tessy was full of gladness when I watched her closely, giving her signs of encouragement and accolades from the sidelines. She shined an endearing smile when she saw me put my finger over my lips, shushing a mother who was trying to talk to me because I was more interested in watching her dance. I watched Tessy give her full attention to her teacher. But when Gina's attention steered away from the group to help a specific girl who needed special instructions, Tessy would glance over at me, innocently waving her hand at me, or she'd awkwardly attempt to do a pirouette in her pink tutu and then peek back at me, awaiting my reaction. Once, when class was over, Tessy shyly took the hand of a little girl, walked her over to me, and said sweetly, "This is my Auntie. She takes care of me because my mommy is sick." Then she reached for my hand, gesturing me to take the little girl's hand in mine.

I liked watching Gina. She was an older dark-haired petite woman who wore cherry-red lipstick and talked with an emotive Italian accent. With the grace and elegance of a ballet dancer, she sauntered about the room, fluttering like a butterfly in between the little girls, instructing and guiding them. Her lean body was sensual, her feet light as air, her arms poised and flowing. Her loveliness inspired me. Being in the dance studio reminded me of my own childhood and the dancer I once was, and I began to wonder when and how my passion and love for dancing had died.

In the late spring, I decided to take a weekly Middle Eastern belly dance class offered at the Louden Nelson Community Center. The kids came to class with me. I thought Tessy might really enjoy it, but neither of them had much of an interest, especially Timmy.

"Why do I have to go to a stupid girl's dance class every week?" he complained, while sitting at the kitchen table doing his homework, after I announced my latest hobby and our new schedule.

"Because it's only offered on Thursday evenings, and there's no one available to watch you while I take the class," I replied, standing at the chopping block slicing vegetables for a salad.

"But I don't wanna go!" he sulked.

"I understand you don't want to. And I don't always want to drive you to Brandon's house or Tae Kwon Do class either. But I do because it's important to you, and you need my help. This is important to me, and I need *your* help," I told him.

In the beginning, I felt a little awkward, even shy in class, standing in the back of the room watching the more confident students fill the first two rows—the ones directly in front of the full-length mirrors. But over time, as I began to learn how to move and sway my body to the sound of the music, I enjoyed expressing myself and the feeling of being alive and free.

On the way home every week, we stopped at the video store. The kids and I worked out an agreement. If they sat quietly on the chairs in the corner of the room tending to their homework or reading a book, or in Timmy's case, playing with his Game Boy, then afterwards, I would take them to the video store where they each picked out a movie for the upcoming weekend. It all worked out in the end. It usually does.

Dad called me late one morning after I had just returned home from a long hike. "I hate to break the news to you dear, but I just received word from Joan's therapist. The doctors and counselors are all in agreement. They feel it's time for Joan to be reunited with her family. It's time to bring the kids back home."

Everything stopped.

I closed my eyes tight and bit down on my lower lip, as I slumped back into the rocking chair in my bedroom. I held my breath and swallowed hard, fighting back the tears.

"Laura? Are you there? Are you okay, dear?" Dad asked in a soft, gentle voice.

I sucked in a sharp, shallow breath and said, "Yep."

"It's time, dear. It's time to bring the children back home to your sister." His words echoed with a cold finality.

My body started to shake and quiver. I released the tight grip on my jaw as I burst out into heaving sobs. Neither of us said a word. Dad sat silent on the other end as I held the phone away from my ear, gripped my queasy stomach, and cried.

After some time, while wiping my tear-stained face, I said, "I don't want to bring them back Dad. I don't want to let them go."

"I know, dear. But you *have* to."

"Can't I fight it?"

"Do you really want to do that to your sister? And the kids? They're *her* children."

"I know, Dad. But, I don't want to give them up."

"I can't even begin to imagine how difficult this is for you. But it'll all work out," were the last words I remember him saying.

After Dad and I said our goodbyes, I sat at my desk and called everyone I knew. I sobbed on the phone with the hollow news to anyone who was available. I didn't want to be alone. I felt like my entire world was collapsing. After I talked with a couple of friends, I called my mother. Much to my surprise, she was home and welcomed my call. She had already heard the news from Joan.

"I'm really happy Joan's recovered. But I don't want to give them back, Mom. I love them so much. I love being a family with them. I'm going to be so lost without them." I cried and cried.

"Oh, Laura. Motherhood can be the most painful job in the world. You've done such a wonderful job for your sister and her children. And now, maybe you're ready for your own family. Maybe it's time for you to have your own children. Something's kept you from that all these years. I know you'll make a wonderful mother. I've always known that, even when you were a little girl. Maybe it's time now, Laura, for you to be a mother."

"But Mom, I love Timmy and Tessy. I want to be *their* mom," I said, insistently.

"But Laura, they're not yours, honey. They're not *your* children."

Children never really do belong to any one. No one does. We come into this world and are handed the fate of being cared for, guided, and if we are fortunate, deeply loved by another. But ultimately we stand on our own. No one is ever free from loss. The wondrous and harsh events of life await us all. My life's longings seemed to bring me toward a moment in time I would not be able to stop. Mirabai, a 15th century Hindu mystic poet, wrote, "The heat of midnight tears will bring you to God." But even still, the emptiness and solitude that soon found their way to me was far greater than I had ever known.

# Emptiness

Early one Sunday morning in June, I woke up alone. It was the second time I'd spent a night without the kids in over a year. They wanted, actually, they had *begged* me to let them go with Briana to her grandmother's house for a sleepover the night before. At first I resisted; I wanted them to myself. I wanted us to stay home for our family movie night. I wanted to wake up the next morning, cook French toast for them, go to church, and spend Sunday afternoon, our family day, going to the beach or the Santa Cruz Boardwalk or bike riding.

But they didn't want to. They wanted *their* life, independent from *our* life, separate from me. I knew my reasons for not wanting them to go were selfish. With incredible accuracy, Timmy saw right through it all and in fact, he called me on it.

"But we don't wanna stay home for family night because *you* want to. We want to be with our friend, Briana."

So I gave in and agreed to their sleepover. I decided to take advantage of my free time and enjoy an evening out. I got dressed up and went out to dinner with a girlfriend, then slept in the following morning. It was wonderful. I didn't feel restricted on how late I should stay out, and I woke up the following morning able to write in my journal uninterrupted. I even rolled out my yoga mat on my bedroom floor and practiced yoga without the kids disrupting me.

But I also got a taste of life without them. When I finally had alone time to myself, I felt an emptiness as wide as the sky inside.

Dad, Joan, and I agreed the kids would finish out the school year and I would return them on June thirtieth, Joan's thirty-first birthday, exactly one year from the day we left. I couldn't stand the thought of them not being in my life, so I decided to move back home. I was the only one in our family who had ever moved away. Dad was thrilled with my decision; it gave him great pleasure knowing I was moving back, even if it would be for an indefinite amount of time.

Once our plans were made and the wheels were in motion, everything happened with a heightened awareness as time ticked forward much too quickly. Everything I did with the kids seemed extraordinarily precious. I savored each and every blessed moment I had with them. Every time Tessy curled up in my arms, I nuzzled her close, breathing in her sweetness, like a mother smelling her newborn. My heart softened watching Timmy's studious face nightly as he leaned over his homework at the kitchen table. Each morning I welled with tears when I dropped them off at school. I felt as if I were in a dream state, sitting in my car, waving goodbye to them as I watched them walk up the long concrete walkway, away from me. It was like a tiny death every morning, as if the end of living were near.

In that last month, everything came to an end: school, Timmy's rec program, dance, chorus, and Tae Kwon Do. I attended every performance with the pride of a peacock. I proudly watched Timmy, when it came his turn to perform for his belt testing ceremony, move his arms and legs in quick snapping motions while dressed in his white dobok. He humbly bowed to his teacher and then to an audience of two hundred, after receiving his new yellow stripes.

I stood tall and clapped the hardest and loudest when Tessy and Mary, a tiny brunette, sang "Feelin' Groovy" for chorus night. They wore matching ankle-length daisy print cotton dresses. They each carried a huge nylon marigold flower umbrella that was almost as big as they were. They twirled the pointy flower on their shoulders as they took turns singing to one another. And I presented Tessy with a bouquet of long-stemmed yellow roses after her dance recital. She had dressed in red spandex shorts and a black sequined halter vest with black fishnet stockings for a cabaret number. We spray-painted her tap shoes fire engine red, and she wore long black satin gloves and a glittery red gangster hat. All nine girls looked as if they were playing musical chairs as they danced around white spindle wooden chairs, tipping their hats to the audience when they completed their performance.

Outwardly I took great pleasure in their successes. On the inside, my heart sobbed big tears watching the days dwindle away, knowing I would never have this time with them ever again.

"Can we have a pool party on our last day of school?" asked Timmy, while discussing our moving plans.

They invited all their classmates to our house on that final day. Michael made sure the pool was packed with colorful new floats and neon-colored water guns for the special event. Even Mr. Andrews, Tessy's teacher, showed up for the celebration with his guitar. After lunch he put on a tall red and white-striped Dr. Seuss Cat in the Hat hat and gathered the twenty children around the patio table. We played sing-alongs and "Name That Tune". The kids tied a red bandana around Sashi's neck, and Mr. Andrew coached her to bark on cue when he played "Bingo". Afterwards, all the kids mobbed Sashi, wanting their picture taken with "Sashi the singing dog".

A certain melancholy set in for me when saying our

goodbyes. I snapped pictures of the kids everywhere we went. We took our final drive down to Los Angeles to say goodbye to their new friends. We spent our last Wednesday afternoon at the farmer's market where, for the very last time, they received caricature balloons from Mr. Twister. On the day before we departed, we spent the afternoon at the Santa Cruz Boardwalk, where Tessy finally got to ride the Giant Dipper roller coaster. For months on end, every time we had visited the boardwalk, she'd prayed she'd reach the fifty-inch marker, but she had always come up a couple of inches short.

"I have an idea," offered Timmy one day, while planning their last boardwalk outing. "Maybe we can buy you a pair of shoes with heels on them so you can reach the line."

So the day before our trip to the boardwalk, the three of us went to Ross and found a pair of white summer chunky sandals with a three-inch heel. We had high hopes she'd finally reach the required minimum height.

On the day of our excursion, as we approached the roller coaster, Timmy said assuringly, "I know you're gonna make it this time, Tessy. I just know it," with tightly crossed fingers.

When we arrived at the roller coaster, there was a long line of people waiting. Timmy was a few steps in front of us and waved us through the crowd until we finally landed in front of the red and green measuring marker. Tessy placed her body up against the marker and with her arms straight down at her side, she gazed at Timmy as he sized up the situation.

"You made it, Tessy!" he exclaimed, with eyes as wide as his smile.

I felt torn up on the inside. I wanted to safely bring the children back into my sister's arms. I wanted Timmy and Tessy to once again be reunited with their beloved mommy and sister. I knew it would bring them great joy to be back home again. I wanted everything to work out and our story to have a happy Hollywood ending. I tried to stay present to the moment and see the positive in the freedom in the future that awaited me. But every day my heart ached with great pain. Our nightly bath routine ceased to exist. Gone were the prayers and lullabies. Our early morning cuddles in bed came to an end. No longer would they peck me on my cheek before jumping out of the car when I dropped them off at school in the morning. The daily chores of making beds, preparing meals, and doing laundry came to a screeching halt. Vanished somewhere in time were our family movie nights, Sunday morning breakfasts, and the most difficult one of all—answering to the call of "Auntie."

It all happened quicker than a breath. In a matter of what seemed like an instant, it was all over.

# *The Return*

We landed at Logan Airport in the late afternoon of my sister's thirty-first birthday. None of us slept a wink on the six-hour plane ride; the kids were too excited. Tessy took the window seat and Timmy sat next to her. They peered out the window once Boston came into view and never took their eyes away as their homeland became more and more real for them.

"We're going to see our mommy," said Tessy, clapping her hands with her eyes lit brighter than the sun.

She wore her favorite dress for the occasion, a short blue spaghetti-strap cotton sundress with large white flowers and a white eyelet hem. She wore her white straw sunhat, but ended up carrying it in her hands most of the time because she had broken the elastic neck string twisting it too tightly while standing in the boarding line at the gate in the San Francisco airport. While on the plane, I silently kissed goodbye the little ones who had fallen deep into my heart. With moist eyes, I sighed listening to them talk about the wonderful things they expected to do as a family once they were together again.

"Hey, Timmy, I bet Mommy will make her special French toast for us tomorrow morning," said Tessy, licking her lips with her tongue.

"Yeah, and maybe Mom will take us to the playground

and Peaceful Meadows for ice-cream, just like we used to," added Timmy.

I was flooded with memories of yesterdays. I smiled remembering Timmy walking around the house in his Tae Kwon Do uniform. When he put that outfit on, he became a different person. Wearing the face of a stone, he'd move his arms and hands in slow circular motion, all the while wearing his adorable gray and white husky plush animal slippers with the pointy ears flapping as he moved. They loved when I played the wicked stepmother after bath time. After they dried off, I'd wrap each of their little bodies in a thick bath towel, pick them up, bring them into my bedroom, and throw them onto my bed while uttering, "My little horrible step-children, I'll get you!" Then I'd tickle them until they screamed, "Stop! No!" Seconds later they'd plead with me, "Do that again, Auntie. *Please.*"

A vast sadness and heavy darkness set in, as I was plagued with memories of moments I knew I would never, ever touch again. During our plane ride, I recited over and over again an Irish prayer our minister Sandy had given me on our last day at church. She handed me a card with a picture of a mother walking hand in hand with her two young children on a burnt orange sunset beach. The prayer read:

> *Mothers and fathers hold their children's hands for*
> *just a little while...And their hearts forever.*

I tried to carry them in my heart, but what I wanted more than anything was to hold their little hands again. The pain of loss cut deep inside me. I tried to find meaning in it all; in the blood that connects us to one another, in the waning moon that controls our destiny. I wondered, *Does our life ever truly belong to us?* I didn't have answers; I only had looming questions that went unanswered for a long, long time.

Once we stepped off the plane, I held Tessy's hand while she toted her purple Pocahontas suitcase, just the way she had when we boarded the plane one year earlier. Timmy, who was wearing his red and navy blue Red Sox jersey along with a Red Sox baseball cap, was already a few steps in front of us. He swung his backpack over his shoulder and stood on his toes when the line in front of us came to a stop, peering through the crowd, looking for signs of his mother.

I had shipped most of their belongings in boxes a few days before we left. Timmy had insisted on carrying his most cherished possessions with him on the plane, just as he had the year before. On the flight to California, it was his *Goosebumps* books that had held his affections. A year later, on the return flight to Boston, it was his Super Nintendo games he cared most about. We walked slowly through the echoing airport tunnel. The children walked with spring in their step, eagerly anticipating their reunion.

As soon as we turned the corner, Joan, Dad, and Lilly came into view and Timmy yelled, "There she is!" pointing his finger straight ahead. Quickly, he turned back to Tessy and said, "Do you see her, Tessy? Do you see her?"

"No, I can't," she said anxiously, as she jumped up into the air. "Where is she?"

"Look, over there. Follow my finger," he told her, pointing through the crowd. "You see? She's standing behind that red rope. See her?"

"Yes! I see her! I see my mommy!" she exclaimed, clapping her hands, wearing a radiant smile.

A moment later, when the line moved a few feet forward, Tessy dropped her luggage, and the two of them ran straight into their mother's arms. Dad stood a few feet behind Joan and

Lilly. His hands were clasped together under his belly with a newspaper tucked under his upper arm. His forehead dripped with sweat from the heat as he beamed a smile watching their reunion. He looked over at me, winked, and stretched out his arm, inviting me in for a hug. I slowly walked past Joan and the kids as they huddled tightly for a long group hug. They were kissing and hugging and crying and laughing, all at the same time. I was half smiling at the sight of their jubilation, but mostly I felt the sadness of my separation from the kids. I nestled myself under Dad's massive arms, resting my head on his chest as I bit my lower lip, fighting back the tears. In that very moment, the presence I had held in Timmy and Tessy's life faded like a long-forgotten dream.

I called Joan and the kids every day. Joan told me she wanted to be with her children, alone, uninterrupted by my presence. As a result, I only saw the kids once a week. But it was all so different. They didn't want to go back in time the way I wanted to. Since I was staying with Dad, Joan dropped the kids off at Dad's apartment for a few hours on Saturday mornings. While sitting on the living room floor in front of the TV late that first morning, I called our Santa Cruz family. After speaking with Michael, I handed the telephone to Timmy, but he shook his head no and said, "I don't wanna talk right now." When I tried to hand the phone to Tessy, she too sat glued to the TV, shaking her head no.

The pain cut deeper the following Saturday morning when we walked out of Dad's apartment to get into his Buick so I could drive them home. Walking along the driveway, I reached for Tessy's hand, but she refused my gesture and ran ahead of me. But what really hurt was when they stopped calling me "Auntie" and instead, for the first time ever, they began calling me "Aunt Laura".

I missed them desperately; their absence from my life felt unnatural and opened an old wound. A long barren silence cut deep and took up residence in my heart. No longer were they under my feet, tugging on my sleeve, asking for my help, or needing me. I longed for our life again. It felt as if it had all been a dream, us being together, and then it was all gone. I couldn't touch our life, or them, any longer. I wasn't sure who I was anymore. I felt separate, lost in the empty moments of long forgotten days. I came to understand first hand what a lonely world it is when we don't have someone to give our love to.

I had a lot more freedom in my life, though my empty days were long. I tried to fill my time as best I could. A week after we arrived home, my friend Kate came for a visit. I was so grateful to have someone or something to fill the void, even if it was only for a little bit of time. Summer was in full swing. We drove down to the Cape for a couple of days. We spent long hours walking barefoot on the white sand dune beaches. We rented bicycles and rode the canal along the seashore. In the sultry summery evenings, we browsed for hours through the quaint local cobblestone shops. I saw families everywhere we went: mothers strolling their babies in carriages, moms and dads bicycling with their kids, families dining in restaurants. A different kind of longing stirred deep in my bones. It was a craving or hunger for something outside myself, something far out of reach.

I attended my cousin Tommy's wedding with Dad and reconnected with family I hadn't seen in years. Everyone asked me questions and was curious to learn about my life. I had absolutely nothing to say. I didn't have a job to speak of, a husband to talk about, or tales of beloved children to share. What's more, I felt unsettled; I didn't have a sense of belonging to anyone or anything and had no plans for my immediate future. A loneliness came and seemed to last forever. I felt lost, hopeless, and alone.

Over my bed in Dad's apartment, I hung Dad's gold-framed AA creed:

*God, grant me the serenity to accept the things I cannot change.*
*The courage to change the things I can.*
*And the wisdom to know the difference.*

I recited it several times every morning upon waking as a way to help find strength to get through each day.

I ran into my former husband Billy at Shaw's Supermarket late one Sunday morning. He had long since remarried and introduced me to his daughter, Amy. She was almost three-years-old and had the same long, dark ringlet curls as her dad. She wore bib jean overalls and white sandals that flashed a soft pink light when she walked. She blushed and hid behind her daddy's leg with her tiny hands holding onto his jeans when he introduced her to me. Billy beamed a brilliant smile for his little girl, a smile I'd never seen in him before. I was happy for him, truly I was, while at the same time, I questioned the choices I had made in my life. I realized for the first time, I was the only one in my life.

For a few months, once a week, Mom and I met for lunch at Christo's, her favorite restaurant. In an obscure corner booth, under the faintly lit glass hanging lights, we sat across from one another, and expressed our silent grievances, which had gone unstated for far too many years. I shared my buried pain and private sorrow when I confessed to her that at the young age of eighteen, I had found myself pregnant. Billy wanted us to marry and have the baby. In fact, he had said a big yes. He wanted me, us, a family, our family—though in the end, he left the decision up to me.

"I couldn't do it Mom. I was so scared. I was so afraid to come to you and Dad and let you know I was pregnant. I didn't want to be a teenage mother, so I had an abortion," I told her through blubbering tears. "And now, after being a mother to Timmy and Tessy, I'd give anything to have had my baby."

She stood up, walked around the table, and sat beside me in the booth. She placed her arm around my shoulders and with a gentle touch, laid my head upon her shoulder as I sobbed in her arms. We cried and held onto one another as we bared more of ourselves to each other.

Every time we met, I disclosed more of my secret self to the woman who birthed my soul. Each time I felt cleansed from the burdens and resentments I had long carried. In the late afternoon following our lunch dates, I found myself taking long walks in the park, being with myself, reflecting and trying to accept and understand the profound loneliness I felt and the deeper meaning in it all. At night, I returned home to Dad's apartment, to the endless silent hours and the enormous hole in my heart.

People often said to me, "It's amazing what you did for your sister and her kids." In time, what I came to realize was the gift they had given me. I'd been wanting someone all my life to find me. By being present with my unresolved childhood wounds, I was beginning to find my way back home, back to myself, back to my own heart.

I cried a lot. I prayed too. I prayed for strength and courage to face the darkest moments of my life. The silence and emptiness were hard. I felt desperate and incredibly lonely. Nothing held my interest. I lost my desire to eat and to be with friends and loved ones. I even lost my passion to hike. I spent days, weeks, months in great despair, grieving my loss like a mother mourning the passing of her beloved child. It was more than a bad moment in my life; it was the dark night of the soul. I felt abandoned by everyone and everything, by a life that was once full of promise and hope.

But in time, being with the silent empty moments of my life gave way to a new beginning. In the midst of my struggles, while wallowing in my aloneness, I had a dream one night. I was sitting in the first row of an empty classroom. I was wearing an elegant milky white saree with gold speckles and trim. The teacher, a tall dark-haired handsome man, sat behind a large glass desk. He was wearing a blue pinstripe Armani suit with a glittering gold necktie. He told me, "Everything's going to be fine in your life. The Soul's work you just completed was to help unify enemy forces that exist inside you and your family. These forces exist in all of us. You not only survived, but you'll go on to have a happier life and the world is now a better place."

I woke up smiling, feeling happy for the first time in months and knew it was time for me to move forward, to be in the mystery of my life once again.

*A Conversation with Laura Maher*

# About the Book

**What is the essence of Auntie Mom?**

It's a universal tale of what happens when any of us are faced with the unexpected challenges life throws us and the transformation and growth that oftentimes occurs along the way. It's my personal experience of a pivotal moment in my life when I found myself suddenly in the role of "parent" for a year to my niece and nephew after my sister suffered a stroke. It was through parenting that I learned how my unresolved childhood losses and longings continued to influence my present day adult life. By bringing awareness to them and working through those painful childhood wounds, I was able to resolve and heal the reasons behind my turbulent relationship with my mother, the abandonment I felt by my father, as well as my fears and ambivalence in embracing motherhood. Mostly I was able to find my way back home to myself, back to my own heart.

**Do you have any favorite scenes in the book?**

I loved the scene when Timmy won a bet for a million dollars. After he collects his reward, he comes running towards me, yelling, "Auntie, you don't ever have to worry again. I'm gonna take care of you from now on. I just won a million dollars!" He believed the money was real and truly wanted to use his winnings to take care of us, his family. The story ends when we go to church the following morning, which happens to be Mother's Day. Church members offer trinkets and stories in honor of their mothers. Timmy offers his newfound winnings, wanting the church to help people in need, like his mom. My heart was so drenched with love for him.

**In the last chapter of the book, you talk about how you felt lost, hopeless, and alone. Can you say a few words about that experience?**

It was an incredibly lonely period in my life. I'd never had the experience of being depressed or feeling despair, but after the kids left my life, I was overwhelmed with an incredible feeling of loneliness and isolation. It was almost unbearable. I couldn't fill that emptiness with anything external like being with family or friends, or engaging with activities I loved like hiking, cooking, and reading. Life at that time had no meaning for me.

**How did you get through it?**

By being present with my experience, by feeling the pain, every aching moment of it. I didn't understand it at that time, but it was a grieving process I was going through. I journaled a lot. In time, I came to accept the situation and move on, though it took quite a bit of time.

**Did you find it difficult to talk about your childhood memories and pain in the book?**

Not really. After I returned the kids to my sister, I spent years processing those childhood wounds through psychotherapy. Then a couple of years before writing the book, I had another round of reexamining those wounds when I completed a master's program in psychology. By the time I wrote the book, I felt healed and complete for the most part.

**Can you say a few words about crisis and transformation?**

I believe the experience I went through during my family's crisis is similar to Joseph Campbell's *The Hero's Journey*. In Campbell's model, one receives the call or invitation to adventure that may come in the form of a crisis, which is a sudden and often traumatic change in one's life. The next step is to enter into the unknown, which is a world full of challenges and even dangers. Along the way, one bears witness to their limitations, they observe their greatest weaknesses, touch their deepest fears, and feel their most vulnerable emotions. By overcoming these obstacles, one transforms himself, meaning there's a dramatic change in their values and in the way they view life. I now see crisis as an opportunity, a stepping-stone for greater spiritual emergence, and a chance for growth. In the process, a part of us must die so a new self can be born. The transformations we undergo oftentimes bring us into greater harmony with ourselves and the world.

**What are your hopes for the book?**

My hope is that the book offers readers self-reflection and inspiration when faced with uncertainty in difficult times. During the year I raised my sister's kids, I didn't know how to pragmatically get us through all the difficult challenges we faced, first with my sister's stroke and then when the kids and I didn't have a home to live in. But everyday I just focused on what needed to get done and miraculously, one thing led to the next, and we were amazingly guided and supported. The generosity and kindness people showed us has always helped me to remember the good that exists in the world.

I also hope the book helps to bridge the gap between women who are childless and children in need. I find it ironic that I decided to care for my sister's children mostly because I didn't want them going into foster care. In the last six years I've been mentoring a young girl who has spent most of her life in foster care and/or group homes. I learned it's estimated over half a million children currently reside in the United States foster care system. I can only hope the book inspires women, especially those who long to express their maternal desires, to give their love, care, and attention to the many kids out there who need it.

# About the Author

**Have you always been a writer?**

No, actually I shied away from both reading and writing beginning in elementary school when I had an embarrassing moment reading in front of the class. That memory surfaced when reading bedtime stories to Timmy and Tessy. I felt embarrassed, even shameful when reading to them. After they returned to their mother, I started exploring different creative mediums like dancing, painting, and writing as a way to understand and heal myself. But there was always this inner voice. That's what I listened to, all my life, my inner voice. It guided me to overcome my shame by learning how to write and eventually, to write my story.

**Can you speak more on that inner voice?**

For me I refer to it as intuition, an instinctive knowing. Some people experience it as a feeling, while for others it's a gut reaction. I believe we all have the ability, though it's more developed in some people than in others. Sometimes for me it comes by way of a dream. Like in the book, I had a dream where I chose to live a carefree, unattached life, rather than care for the kids. When I woke up, I began missing the kids fiercely and felt overwhelmed by the fear of losing them. A day or two later, I received a call from my sister stating she wanted her children back. I believe that inner voice is always directing and guiding my life.

## What books and authors most influenced you?

I loved Barack Obama's, *Dreams from My Father*. I loved that Obama went back to his roots in an attempt to understand who he was. I love everything by Mary Karr. I especially love her candor. When I read Anne Lamott's *Traveling Mercies* years ago, I knew someday I would write my story. In general, I love reading personal narratives.

## What preparations did you make to write your story?

I took a year off to write my thesis on *Transformation Through Crisis,* for my master's program. A week after I graduated, I hit my head and suffered a slight concussion. There was this story in my head that I couldn't let go of, so I wrote it down, and I didn't stop writing. The stories, the scenes, the feelings, all came through. I also read the journals I wrote while raising the kids and looked at all the photographs I took during that year. The journals and photos helped spark certain memories that allowed me to describe particular scenes I had long forgotten.

## Can you talk about your experience of writing your memoir? Did you learn anything?

I learned that writing my story offered me an opportunity to reflect on my life. It was a cathartic process, meaning I felt cleansed and healed by it. I came to terms with some of the decisions I had made in my life and who I came to be as a person. I loved learning that when Bill Clinton was in the process of writing his memoir, he said he found it to be such an illuminating process, reviewing the various episodes of his life, crafting them into a narrative form, culminating in the composite of who he'd become. I understood first-hand what he experienced and believe it to be a valuable tool for anyone.

# Acknowledgements

Bringing this book into fruition would not have been possible without the help of many hands. First and foremost, I'd like to thank my writing group: Jean-Marie Murphy, Carol Benson, Ravi Nathwani, Doug Greene, and Josh Cohen. Your insights, support, and guidance in helping me to find the present moment have been invaluable.

A heartfelt thanks goes out to my dear friend Shanti Cliff who patiently read every word of my manuscript, and who truly understood the story I wanted to tell.

And to Carol Sun who devoured every word. Although she claims to be a "hard critic", her words were kind and suggestions brilliant.

I'd like to say a special thank you to Peter Clarke for helping me to discover my voice. You will always hold a giant place in my heart.

I am indebted to my family. How lucky I am to have a father who has always encouraged me to live life and who models the values of integrity, honesty, and taking responsibility. I am proud to be your daughter. And for my mother, you've been my biggest cheerleader and taught me early on "to go for it". I love you dearly.

I am in deep gratitude to my one and only sister, who urged me to share my truth. Sisterhood is long term. At the end of our life, I know we will be the one constant for each other. You continue to teach me what it means to be a sister as well as a friend.

Lots of thanks to my great friend Doug Greene whose creative direction, enthusiasm, and loyalty is nothing less than inspiring.

Finally, a few words to Timmy and Tessy. We have walked a few roads together. I am humbled by the gift of loving you. Your presence in my life has truly been one of life's greatest treasures.

# The Author

LAURA MAHER was born and raised in Massachusetts. She has a master's degree in integral psychology from JFK University. *Auntie Mom* is her literary debut. She lives in Northern California.

You can visit her online at www.AuntieMomBook.com